Also by Jim Loewen

Lies Across America: What Our Historic Sites Get Wrong

Lies My Teacher Told Me:
Everything Your American History Textbook Got Wrong

The Mississippi Chinese: Between Black and White

Mississippi: Conflict and Change (with Charles Sallis, et al.)

Social Science in the Courtroom

The Truth About Columbus:
A Subversively True Poster Book for a Dubiously Celebratory Occasion

Sundown Towns

A Hidden Dimension of American Racism

James W. Loewen

A Touchstone Book
Published by Simon & Schuster
New York   London   Toronto   Sydney

 TOUCHSTONE
Rockefeller Center
1230 Avenue of the Americas
New York, NY 10020

Originally published in the United States in 2005 by The New Press.

Published by arrangement with The New Press.

First Touchstone Edition 2006

TOUCHSTONE and colophon are registered trademarks
of Simon & Schuster, Inc.

For information regarding special discounts for bulk purchases, please contact Simon & Schuster Special Sales at 1-800-456-6798 or business@simonandschuster.com.

Manufactured in the United States of America

10 9 8 7 6 5 4 3 2 1

The Library of Congress has cataloged The New Press edition as follows:

Loewen, James W.
Sundown towns : a hidden dimension of American racism / James W. Loewen.
p. cm.
Includes biographical references and index.
ISBN 1–56584–887-X (hc)
1. African Americans—Segregation. 2. Cities and towns—United States. 3. Suburbs—United States. 4. City and town life—United States. 5. Suburban life—United States. 6. United States—History, Local 7. Discrimination in housing—United States. 8. Racism—United States. 9. United States—Race relations. I. Title.

E185.615.L577 2005
363.5'5'0973091732—dc22   2005043855

ISBN-13: 978-0-7432-9448-5 (pbk.)
ISBN-10:   0-7432-9448-3 (pbk.)

Contents

Part V: Effects of Sundown Towns

Part VI: The Present and Future of Sundown Towns

Note to the Reader

Readers may need to brace themselves to deal with the language they will meet in this book. I shall not soften it by using *n-word* or other euphemisms. People said what they said and wrote what they wrote; their language is part of the story. Indeed, this language is part of what makes sundown towns distinctive, so I could not tell their story honestly while expurgating the language.

Younger readers need to understand that *Negro* was the standard term used to refer to African Americans before about 1972, by blacks as well as whites, and connoted no disrespect. Before about 1950, writers did not always capitalize *Negro*, although since it was parallel to *Caucasian,* they should have. I have taken the liberty of capitalizing *negro* in quoted sources from these earlier years. When writers used *negro* even after 1972—long after most authors had converted to *black* or *African American*—I have left *negro* uncapitalized. After 1972, writers who persist in using *negro* demonstrate either a deliberate refusal to use *black* or to capitalize *Negro* or an appalling ignorance of correct usage, which I would not want to mask from my readers. Such writing would be uncommon in a multiracial town by 1974.

Occasionally I place quotation marks around a name at first occurrence, indicating that the name is fictitious. Some other names have been omitted or disguised, to avoid any repercussion to people who kindly shared information with me, because the informant asked not to be identified, or because I did not know them.

Notes placed in the midst of paragraphs are content footnotes. Reference footnotes come at the end of paragraphs. In the references, web sites are listed without http:// or www. and are followed by the date accessed. Names followed by dates—Jane Doe, 9/2002—refer to interviews in person or by phone.

I don't footnote the U.S. census; finding population figures there is not hard and not eased much by citations. In the 2000 census I used the single-race counts, because it is not clear how an individual who states two or three races on the census form identifies in society, because the census uses single-race data for important tables such as "households," and because only 2.4% of census respondents chose more than one race.

Often I quote from e-mails. Unfortunately, not to bother to write e-mails in correct English has become conventional, perhaps because this ephemeral electronic form is viewed as intermediate between talking and writing. Since quoting changes the form to traditional written, I have usually taken the liberty of correcting minor lapses in spelling and grammar in e-mails.

PART I

Introduction

1

The Importance of Sundown Towns

"Is it true that 'Anna' stands for 'Ain't No Niggers Allowed'?" I asked at the convenience store in Anna, Illinois, where I had stopped to buy coffee.

"Yes," the clerk replied. "That's sad, isn't it," she added, distancing herself from the policy. And she went on to assure me, "That all happened a long time ago."

"I understand [racial exclusion] is still going on?" I asked.

"Yes," she replied. "That's sad."

—conversation with clerk, Anna, Illinois, October 2001

ANNA IS A TOWN of about 7,000 people, including adjoining Jonesboro. The twin towns lie about 35 miles north of Cairo, in southern Illinois. In 1909, in the aftermath of a horrific nearby "spectacle lynching," Anna and Jonesboro expelled their African Americans. Both cities have been all-white ever since.[1] Nearly a century later, "Anna" is still considered by its residents and by citizens of nearby towns to mean "Ain't No Niggers Allowed," the acronym the convenience store clerk confirmed in 2001.

It is common knowledge that African Americans are not allowed to live in Anna, except for residents of the state mental hospital and transients at its two motels. African Americans who find themselves in Anna and Jonesboro after dark—the majority-black basketball team from Cairo, for example—have sometimes been treated badly by residents of the towns, and by fans and students of Anna-Jonesboro High School. Towns such as Anna and Jonesboro are often called "sundown towns," owing to the signs that many of them formerly sported at their corporate limits—signs that usually said "Nigger, Don't Let the Sun Go Down on You in __." Anna-Jonesboro had such signs on Highway 127 as recently as the 1970s. These communities were also known as "sunset towns" or, in the Ozarks, "gray towns." In the East, although many communities excluded African Americans, the term "sundown town" itself was rarely used. Residents of all-white suburbs also usually avoided the term, though not the policy.

Sundown Towns Are Almost Everywhere

A sundown town is any organized jurisdiction that for decades kept African Americans or other groups from living in it and was thus "all-white" on purpose.[2] There is a reason for the quotation marks around "all-white": requiring towns to be literally all-white in the census—no African Americans at all—is inappropriate, because many towns clearly and explicitly defined themselves as sundown towns but allowed one black household as an exception.[3] Thus an all-white town may include nonblack minorities and even a tiny number of African Americans.

It turns out that Anna and Jonesboro are not unique or even unusual. Beginning in about 1890 and continuing until 1968, white Americans established thousands of towns across the United States for whites only. Many towns drove out their black populations, then posted sundown signs. (Portfolio 7 shows an example.) Other towns passed ordinances barring African Americans after dark or prohibiting them from owning or renting property; still others established such policies by informal means, harassing and even killing those who violated the rule. Some sundown towns similarly kept out Jews, Chinese, Mexicans, Native Americans, or other groups.

Independent sundown towns range from tiny hamlets such as De Land, Illinois (population 500), to substantial cities such as Appleton, Wisconsin (57,000 in 1970).[4] Sometimes entire counties went sundown, usually when their county seat did. Independent sundown towns were soon joined by "sundown suburbs," which could be even larger: Levittown, on Long Island, had 82,000 residents in 1970, while Livonia, Michigan, and Parma, Ohio, had more than 100,000. Warren, a suburb of Detroit, had a population of 180,000 including just 28 minority families, most of whom lived on a U.S. Army facility.[5]

Outside the traditional South—states historically dominated by slavery, where sundown towns are rare—*probably a majority of all incorporated places kept out African Americans.* If that sentence startles, please suspend disbelief until Chapter 3, which will show that Illinois, for example, had 671 towns and cities with more than 1,000 people in 1970, of which 475—71%—were all-white in census after census.[6] Chapter 3 will prove that almost all of these 475 were sundown towns. There is reason to believe that more than half of all towns in Oregon, Indiana, Ohio, the Cumberlands, the Ozarks, and diverse other areas were also all-white on purpose. Sundown *suburbs* are found from Darien, Connecticut, to La Jolla, California, and are even more prevalent; indeed, most suburbs began life as sundown towns.

Sundown towns also range across the income spectrum. In 1990, the median owner-occupied house in Tuxedo Park, perhaps the wealthiest suburb of New York City, was worth more than $500,000 (the highest category in the census). So was the median house in Kenilworth, the richest suburb of Chicago. The median house in Pierce City, in southwestern Missouri, on the other hand, was worth just $29,800 and in Zeigler, in southern Illinois, just $21,900. All four towns kept out African Americans for decades.

This History Has Been Hidden

Even though sundown towns were everywhere, almost no literature exists on the topic.[7] No book has ever been written about the making of all-white towns in America.[8] Indeed, this story is so unknown as to deserve the term *hidden.* Most Americans have no idea such towns or counties exist, or they think such things happened mainly in the Deep South. Ironically, the traditional South has almost no sundown towns. Mississippi, for instance, has no more than 6, mostly mere hamlets, while Illinois has no fewer than 456, as Chapter 3 will show.

Even book-length studies of individual sundown towns rarely mention their exclusionary policies. Local historians omit the fact intentionally, knowing that it would reflect badly on their communities if publicized abroad. I read at least 300 local histories—some of them elaborate coffee-table books—about towns whose sundown histories I had confirmed via detailed oral histories, but only about 1 percent of these mentioned their town's racial policies. In conversation, however, the authors of these commemorative histories were often more forthcoming, showing that they knew about the policy but didn't care to disclose it in print.

Social scientists and professional historians often have done no better in their books. During the Depression, for instance, Malcolm Brown and John Webb wrote *Seven Stranded Coal Towns,* a report for the federal government about towns in southern Illinois. All seven were sundown towns—most still are—yet the authors never mention that fact. In 1986, anthropologist John Coggeshall wrote about thirteen southern Illinois communities; most were probably sundown towns when he wrote; I have confirmed at least five. Yet he never mentions the topic. In *Toward New Towns for America,* C. S. Stein treats Radburn, New Jersey; "the Greens"—Greenbelt, Maryland, near Washington, DC; Greenhills, Ohio, near Cincinnati; and Greendale, Wisconsin, southwest of Milwaukee—planned towns built by the FDR administration; and several other planned communities, all sundown towns, without ever mentioning race. This takes some doing; about Radburn, for example, Stein details the first residents' occupations, religious denominational member-ships, educational backgrounds, and incomes, without once mentioning that all of them were white—and were required to be. Lewis Atherton's *Main Street on the Middle Border* treats small towns across the Midwest but makes no mention of sundown towns or indeed of African Americans or race rela-tions in any context.[9]

Historians and sociologists may have omitted the fact because they sim-ply did not know about sundown towns. For example, several historians as-sured me that no town in Wisconsin ever kept out or drove out African Americans. James Danky, librarian at the Wisconsin Historical Society, whose book on the black press in America is the standard reference, wrote:

> I have checked with three of my most knowledgeable colleagues and there is consensus, we do not know of any such towns in Wisconsin. Clearly the Badger State has a full supply of racism, just no such towns or counties. I believe you have found such entities elsewhere, it is just that I think that it is a small category, at least in terms of being formally established.

Later, Danky was surprised and intrigued to learn I had confirmed 9 sun-down towns in Wisconsin and 194—no "small category"—in neighboring Illinois. Across the northern United States, many social scientists and histori-ans have gone slack-jawed when hearing details of community-wide exclusion from towns and counties in their state, lasting at least into the late twentieth century.[10]

Overlooking sundown towns stands in sharp contrast to the attention be-stowed upon that other violent and extralegal race relations practice: lynch-ing. The literature on lynching is vast, encompassing at least 500 and perhaps thousands of volumes; at this point we have at least one book for every ten confirmed lynchings. Still the books keep coming; Amazon.com listed 209 for sale in 2005. Yet lynchings have ceased in America.[11] Sundown towns, on the other hand, continue to this day.

Sundown towns arose during a crucial era of American history, 1890–1940, when, after the gains of the Civil War and Reconstruction eras, race relations systematically grew worse. Since the 1955 publication of

C. Vann Woodward's famous book, *The Strange Career of Jim Crow,* historians of the South have recognized that segregation became much stricter after 1890. No longer could African Americans vote; no longer could they use the restaurants and public parks that whites used; even streetcars and railroad waiting rooms now put up screens or signs to isolate blacks in separate sections. African Americans were also beset by violence, as lynchings rose to their highest point.[12] However, most Americans have no idea that race relations *worsened* between 1890 and the 1930s. As Edwin Yoder Jr. wrote in 2003 in the *Washington Post,* "Notwithstanding the brilliant revisionist works of the late C. Vann Woodward, few Americans even remotely grasp the earthquake of 1890–1901 that overthrew biracial voting in the South.[13]

This backlash against African Americans was not limited to the South but was national. Neither the public nor most historians realize that the same earthquake struck the North, too. Woodward actually did; he wrote in the preface to the second edition of his classic that the only reason he did not treat the worsening of race relations in the North was because "my own competence does not extend that far." Unfortunately, except for a handful of important monographs on individual states and locales, few historians have tried to fill the gap in the half century since.[14] Thus they missed one of the most appalling and widespread racial practices of them all: sundown towns. While African Americans never lost the right to vote in the North (although there were gestures in that direction), they did lose the right to live in town after town, county after county.[15]

My Own Ignorance

Initially, I too thought sundown towns, being so extreme, must be extremely rare. Having learned of perhaps a dozen sundown towns and counties—Anna and Edina; Cicero and Berwyn, suburbs of Chicago; Darien, Connecticut, a suburb of New York City; Cedar Key, Florida; Forsyth County, Georgia; Alba and Vidor, Texas; and two or three others—I imagined there might be 50 such towns in the United States. I thought a book about them would be easy to research and write. I was wrong.

I began my on-site research in Illinois, for the simple reason that I grew up there, in Decatur, in the center of the state. Coming of age in central Illinois, however, I never asked why the little towns clustered about my home city had no black residents. After all, I reasoned, some communities are not on major highways, rivers, or rail lines; are not near African American population concentrations; and have not offered much in the way of employment. Probably they never attracted African American residents. I had no idea that *almost all* all-white towns and counties in Illinois were all-white on purpose.

The idea that intentional sundown towns were everywhere in America, or at least everywhere in the Midwest, hit me between the eyes two years into this research—on October 12, 2001. That evening I was the headliner at the Decatur Writers Conference. It was an interesting homecoming, because at the end of my address, I mentioned my ongoing research on sundown towns and invited those who knew something about the subject to come forward and talk with me. In response, a throng of people streamed to the front to tell me about sundown towns they knew of in central Illinois. Moweaqua (2000 population 1,923, 0 African Americans) was all-white on purpose, two people said. Nearby Assumption (1,261, 0 African Americans) was also a sundown town, except for its orphanage, Kemmerer Village, and the few African American children there often had a hard time in the Assumption school because of their color. An Illinoisian who "grew up on a farm just west of Decatur and attended high school in Niantic," a hamlet just west of Decatur (738, 0 African Americans), wrote later, "I had always heard that it was against the law for blacks to stay in Niantic overnight. Supposedly, when the railroad section crew was in the area, they would have to pull the work train, with its sleeping quarters for the section hands, out on the main track for the night." Another person confirmed the railroad story, and two others agreed separately that Niantic kept out black people, so I had to conclude that Niantic's population was all-white not because it was so small, but because African Americans were not permitted. Still others came down with information about De Land, Maroa, Mt. Zion, Pana, Villa Grove, and a dozen other nearby towns.

That evening in Decatur revolutionized my thinking. I now perceived that in the normal course of human events, most and perhaps all towns would *not* be all-white. Racial exclusion was required. "If they did not have such a policy," observed an African American resident of Du Quoin, Illinois, about the all-white towns around Du Quoin, "surely blacks would be *in* them." I came to understand that he was right. "If people of color aren't around," writes commentator Tim Wise, "there's a reason, having something to do with history, and exclusion. . . ."[16]

Though mind-boggling to me, this insight proved hardly new. As early as 1858, before the dispersal of African Americans throughout the North prompted by the Civil War, the *Wyandotte Herald* in Wyandotte, in southeastern Michigan, stated, "Wyandotte is again without a single colored inhabitant, something remarkable for a city of over 6,000 people." Even then, the *Herald* understood that a city of over 6,000 people was "remarkable" for being all-white. We shall see that a series of riots and threats was required to keep Wyandotte white over the years.[17]

Later, after slavery ended, African Americans moved throughout America, making it "remarkable" even for smaller towns to be all-white. The anonymous author of *History of Lower Scioto Valley*, south of Columbus, Ohio, writing in 1884, recognized this in discussing Waverly, a sundown town since before the Civil War:

> In 1875 a local census showed Waverly to have 1,279 inhabitants. . . . It will be seen that the fact of Waverly's not having a single colored resident is a rare mark of distinction for a town of its size. And what makes the fact more remarkable, there never has been a Negro or mulatto resident of the place.[18]

Sundown Towns Are Recent

In 1884, it was "a rare mark of distinction" for a town the size of Waverly to be all-white. A few years later, however, beginning around 1890 and lasting until at least 1968, towns throughout Ohio and most other states began to emulate the racial policy of places like Wyandotte and Waverly. Most independent sundown towns expelled their black residents, or agreed not to admit any, between 1890 and 1940. Sundown suburbs arose still later, between 1900 and 1968. By the middle of the twentieth century, it was no longer rare for towns the size of Waverly to be all-white. It was common, and usually it was on purpose.

So sundown towns are not only widespread, but also relatively recent. Except for a handful of places such as Wyandotte and Waverly, most towns did not go sundown during slavery, before the Civil War, or during Reconstruction. On the contrary, blacks moved everywhere in America between 1865 and 1890. African Americans reached every county of Montana. More than 400 lived in Michigan's Upper Peninsula. City neighborhoods across the country were fairly integrated, too, even if black inhabitants were often servants or gardeners for their white neighbors.

Between 1890 and the 1930s, however, all this changed. By 1930, although its white population had increased by 75%, the Upper Peninsula was home to only 331 African Americans, and 180 of them were inmates of the Marquette State Prison. Eleven Montana counties had no blacks at all. Across the country, city neighborhoods grew more and more segregated. Most astonishing, from California to Minnesota to Long Island to Florida, whites mounted little race riots against African Americans, expelling entire black communities or intimidating and keeping out would-be newcomers.

The Role of Violence

Whenever a town had African American residents and no longer does, we should seek to learn how and why they left. Expulsions and prohibitions often lurk behind the census statistics. Vienna, a town in southern Illinois, provides a rather recent example. In 1950, Vienna had 1,085 people, including a black community of long standing, dating to the Civil War. In the 1950 census, African Americans numbered 34; additional black families lived just outside Vienna's city limits. Then in the summer of 1954, two black men beat up a white grandmother and allegedly tried to rape her teenage granddaughter. The grandmother eventually died, and "every [white] man in town was deputized" to find the culprits, according to a Vienna resident in 2004. The two men were apprehended; in the aftermath, whites sacked the entire black community. "They burned the houses," my informant said. "The blacks literally ran for their lives." The *Vienna Times* put it more sedately: "The three remaining buildings on the South hill in the south city limits of Vienna were destroyed by fire about 4:30 o'clock Monday afternoon." The report went on to tell that the state's attorney and circuit judge later addressed a joint meeting of the Vienna city council and Johnson County commissioners, "telling them of the loss sustained by the colored people." Both bodies "passed a resolution condemning the acts of vandalism" and promised to pay restitution to those who lost their homes and belongings. Neither body invited the black community to return, and no one was ever convicted of the crime of driving them out. In the 2000 census, Vienna's population of 1,234 included just 1 African American.[19]

Violence also lay beneath the surface of towns that showed no sudden decline in black residents, never having had any. In 1951, for example, a Chicago bus driver, Harvey Clark, a veteran, tried to move into an apartment in suburban Cicero. First, the police stopped him by force, according to a report by social scientist William Gremley:

> As he arrived at the building with the moving van, local police officials, including the Cicero police chief, stopped him from entering. When he protested, they informed him he could not move in without a "permit." Clark argued in vain against this edict and finally telephoned his solicitor, who assured him that

there was no provision in local, state, or federal laws for any such "permit." The police officials then bluntly ordered him and the van away, threatening him with arrest if he failed to comply with their demand. Clark then left, after being man-handled and struck.

Two weeks later, with help from the NAACP, Clark got an injunction barring the Cicero police from interfering with his moving in and ordering them "to afford him full protection from any attempt to so restrain him." As he moved in, a month after his first attempt, whites stood across the street and shouted racial epithets. That evening, a large crowd gathered, shouting and throwing stones to break the windows in the apartment Clark had just rented. Prudently, the Clark family did not occupy the apartment. The next night, the mob attacked the building, looted the Clarks' apartment as well as some adjoining flats, threw the Clarks' furniture and other belongings out the window, and set them afire in the courtyard below. Local police stood by and watched.[20]

The following night, a mob of 3,500 gathered and rioted. According to a summary by Peter and Mort Bergman, "Gov. Adlai Stevenson called out the National Guard, and 450 guardsmen and 200 Cicero and Cook County police quelled the disorder; 72 persons were arrested, 60 were charged, 17 people were hospitalized." Violence like this happened repeatedly in Cicero and adjacent Berwyn. In the 1960s, a white mob stoned members of the Congress of Racial Equality (CORE) marching through Cicero supporting open housing. Whites in Cicero beat seventeen-year-old African American Jerome Huey to death in the summer of 1966. In 1987, Norbert Blei, a Cicero resident, wrote *Neighborhood,* a warm memoir about the city. He told how an African American family

> "almost" moved into Cicero on West 12th Place last spring. But they didn't make it. The black family said that they didn't know the home they bought was in Cicero. They thought it was in Chicago. But Cicero reminded them with gas-filled bottles and shots in the dark. "The area is well-secured," said Cicero's council president, John Karner, after the incendiary incident.

So far as I know, no one was ever convicted in Cicero or Vienna.[21]

This is not ancient history. Many victims of Vienna's ethnic cleansing are still alive; some even return to Vienna from time to time to obtain birth certificates or transact other business.[22] The perpetrators and the victims of the

1987 Cicero incident still live. Moreover, African Americans who tried to move into other sundown suburbs and towns have had trouble as recently as 2004, as later chapters will tell.

Across America, at least 50 towns, and probably many more than that, drove out their African American populations violently. At least 16 did so in Illinois alone. In the West, another 50 or more towns drove out their Chinese American populations.[23] Many other sundown towns and suburbs used violence to keep out blacks or, sometimes, other minorities.

Sundown Nation

Sundown towns are no minor matter. To this day, African Americans who know about sundown towns concoct various rules to predict and avoid them. In Florida, for instance, any town or city with "Palm" in its name was thought to be especially likely to keep out African Americans. In Indiana, it was any jurisdiction with a color in its name, such as Brownsburg, Brownstown, Brown County, Greenfield, Greenwood, or Vermillion County—and indeed, all were sundown locales. Across the United States, African Americans are still understandably wary of towns with "white" in their name, such as Whitesboro, Texas; White City, Kansas; White Hall, Arkansas; Whitefish Bay, Wisconsin; and Whiteland, Whitestown, and White County, Indiana—and again, all the foregoing communities probably kept out African Americans. So have a number of towns named for idealistic concepts—Equality, Illinois; New Harmony, Indiana; Liberty, Tennessee, and the like. Actually, most places with "white" in their name were named after someone (or some fish) named "White"; these sundry rules "work" only because *most* communities were sundown towns.

Millions of Americans—including many of our country's leaders—live in or grew up in sundown towns and suburbs. An interesting way to see the ubiquity of these towns is to examine the backgrounds of all northern candidates for president nominated by the two major parties since the twentieth century began and sundown towns became common.[24] Of the 27 candidates for whom I could readily distinguish the racial policies of their hometowns, one-third were identified with sundown towns. Starting at the beginning of the century, these include Republican William McKinley, who grew up in Niles, Ohio, where "a sign near the Erie Depot," according to historian William Jenkins, "warned 'niggers' that they had better not 'let the sun set on their heads.' " McKinley defeated Democrat William Jennings Bryan, who grew up in Salem, Illinois, which for decades "had signs on each main road going into town, telling the blacks, that they were not allowed in town after sundown," according to Ed Hayes, who graduated from Salem High School in 1969. Teddy Roosevelt was most identified with Cove Neck, a tiny upper-class peninsula on Long Island that incorporated partly to keep out undesir-ables, including African Americans, requiring large building lots. As late as 1990, its small black population consisted overwhelmingly of live-in maids. In 1920, Warren G. Harding ran his famous "front porch campaign" from his family home in Marion, Ohio; a few months before, Marion was the scene of an ethnic cleansing as whites drove out virtually every African American. Ac-cording to Harding scholar Phillip Payne, "As a consequence, Marion is an overwhelming[ly] white town to this date [2002]." Herbert Hoover grew up in a part of Iowa that may have gotten rid of its blacks around that time, but I cannot confirm his hometown as a sundown town.[25] Wendell Willkie's father was mayor of Elwood, Indiana, a sundown town that is still all-white today; Willkie went to Elwood in 1940 to deliver his speech accepting the Republi-can nomination. Owosso, Michigan, briefly became mildly notorious as a sun-down town in 1944 and 1948 because Thomas Dewey, Republican candidate for president, grew up there. But Democrats couldn't make too much of that fact, especially in 1948, because their own candidate, Harry Truman, also grew up in a sundown town, Lamar, Missouri. Reporter Morris Milgram pointed out that Lamar "was a Jim Crow town of 3,000, without a single Negro family. When I had spoken about this with leading citizens of Lamar . . . they told me, all using the word 'n——r,' that colored people weren't wanted in Lamar." Another Democrat, Lyndon Johnson, grew up in Johnson City, Texas, probably a sundown town.[26] The trend continues to the present: George W. Bush lived for years in Highland Park, a sundown suburb of Dal-las; so did his vice president, Dick Cheney, from 1995 until he moved to Washington to take office.[27] The first African American to buy a home in Highland Park did so only in June 2003. In all, nine of America's presidential candidates since 1900 grew up in probable sundown towns and suburbs, eighteen came from towns where blacks could live, and five from towns[28] whose policies I haven't been able to identify.[29]

Besides presidents, such famous Americans as public speaker Dale Carnegie (Maryville, Missouri), folksinger Woody Guthrie (Okemah, Okla-homa), Senator Joe McCarthy (Appleton, Wisconsin), etiquette czar Emily Post (Tuxedo Park, New York), and architect Frank Lloyd Wright (Oak Park, Illinois) grew up in towns that kept out African Americans. So did novelists Ernest Hemingway (Oak Park), Edna Ferber (Appleton), and James Jones (Robinson, Illinois), although as far as I can tell, they never mentioned the matter in their writing. I do not know if apple pie was invented in a sundown town, but Spam (Austin, Minnesota), Kentucky Fried Chicken (Corbin, Kentucky), and Heath Bars (Robinson) were. Other signature American edibles such as Krispy Kreme doughnuts (Effingham, Illinois[30]) and Tootsie Rolls (West Lawn, Chicago) also come from sundown communities. Tarzan may have lived in "darkest Africa," but he was born in one sundown town (Oak Park, home of Edgar Rice Burroughs), and the proceeds from his wildly successful novels and movies underwrote Burroughs's creation of another (Tarzana, California).[31] The highest-grossing movie of all time (in constant dollars), *Gone with the Wind,* was made in a sundown town, Culver City, California, from which vantage point producer David Selznick was baffled by petitions from African Americans concerned about the racism in its screenplay.[32] *Gentleman's Agreement,* on the other hand, the only feature film to treat sundown towns seriously, was made in Los Angeles.[33]

Chapter 3, "The Great Retreat," will show that large cities like Los Angeles could not exclude blacks completely—the task was simply too daunting—although residents of New York City, Fort Wayne, Tulsa, and several other cities tried. Nevertheless, whole sections of cities did keep out African Americans and sometimes other groups. Although this book doesn't usually treat "mere" neighborhoods, some sundown neighborhoods are huge. West Lawn in Chicago, for instance, has its own Chamber of Commerce, whose executive director brags that it is "a small town in a big city." It is also the birthplace of the Dove ice cream bar and the Tucker automobile. According to reporter Steve Bogira, in 1980 West Lawn had 113,000 whites and just 111 African Americans. Every large city in the United States has its all-white neighborhoods, all-white by design; certainly the West End of Decatur, where I grew up, was that way. All too many small towns, meanwhile, if they are interracial at all, still consist of sundown neighborhoods on one side, overwhelmingly black neighborhoods on the other, and the business district or a railroad in between. So sundown neighborhoods form another major part of the problem.[34]

Why Dwell On It Now?

Since 1969, I have been studying how Americans remember their past, especially their racial past. Sometimes audiences or readers ask, "Why do you insist on dredging up the abominations in our past?" About sundown towns in particular, some people have suggested that we might all be happier and better off *not* knowing about them. "Why focus on that?" asked an old African American man in Colp, in southern Illinois, in 2001, when he learned I was studying the sundown towns that surrounded Colp in every direction. "That's done with."[35]

I thought about his suggestion seriously. After all, during the 1980s and 1990s, many communities relaxed their prohibitions and accepted at least one or two black families, sometimes many more. But I concluded there were several reasons why the sad story of sundown towns should not be kept out of view.

First—and most basically—it happened. Our country *did* do that. Surely the fact that since about 1890, thousands of towns across the United States kept out African Americans, while others excluded Jewish, Chinese, Japanese, Native, or Mexican Americans, is worth knowing. So is the panoply of methods whites employed to accomplish this end. I hope this book prompts readers to question all-white communities everywhere, rather than take them for granted. Whenever the census shows that a town or county has been all-white or overwhelmingly white for decades, we do well to investigate further, since across the nation, most all-white towns were that way intentionally. Telling the truth about them is the right thing to do.

It is also true that the powers that be don't want us to learn about their policy of exclusion and have sometimes tried to suppress the knowledge. The truth about sundown towns implicates the powers that be. The role played by governments regarding race relations can hardly be characterized as benign or even race-neutral. From the towns that passed sundown ordinances, to the county sheriffs who escorted black would-be residents back across the county line, to the states that passed laws enabling municipalities to zone out "undesirables," to the federal government—whose lending and insuring policies from the 1930s to the 1960s *required* sundown neighborhoods and suburbs—our governments openly favored white supremacy and helped to create and maintain all-white communities. So did most of our banks, realtors, and police chiefs. If public relations offices, Chambers of Commerce, and local historical societies don't want us to know something, perhaps that something is worth learning. After all, how can we deal with something if we cannot even face it?

There are other reasons to incorporate sundown towns into our accounts of our nation's past. "I am anxious for this book," a high school history teacher in Pennsylvania wrote.

> I tend to collect evidence for my students that racism and discrimination still exist. Many like to pass it off as a part of the distant (before they were born) past, thus no further energy or thought need be expended on the issue!

Chronicling the sundown town movement teaches us that something significant has been left out of the broad history of race in America as it is usually taught. It opens a door into an entire era that America has kept locked away in a closet. I hope that *Sundown Towns* will transform Americans' understanding of race relations in the North during the first two-thirds of the twentieth century. Realizing that blatant racial exclusion increased during the first half of the twentieth century and in many places continues into the twenty-first can help mobilize Americans today to expend energy to end these practices.[36]

Many people wonder why African Americans have made so little progress, given that 140 years have passed since slavery ended. They do not understand that in some ways, African Americans lived in better and more integrated conditions in the 1870s and 1880s, that residential segregation then grew worse until about 1968, and that it did not start to decrease again until the 1970s and 1980s, well after the Civil Rights Movement ended. Recovering the memory of the *increasing* oppression of African Americans during the first half of the twentieth century can deepen our understanding of the role racism has played in our society and continues to play today.

Sundown Towns Persist

In other spheres of race relations, America has made great strides. The attention given to southern segregation—not just by historians but, more importantly, by the Civil Rights Movement and the courts, beginning in 1954—ended its more appalling practices. Whites, blacks, and other races ride the same subways, buses, trains, and planes. Americans of all backgrounds work together in offices, restaurants, factories, and the military. Universities, north and south, now enroll African American undergraduates; some even compete for them. Republican as well as Democratic administrations include African Americans in important positions as a matter of course. We have made far less progress, however, regarding where we live. Aided by neglect, the number of sundown towns and suburbs continued to grow after 1954, peaking around 1968. Many sundown towns had not a single black household as late as the 2000 census, and some still openly exclude to this day.

Many whites still feel threatened at the prospect of African American neighbors—maybe not just one, but of any appreciable number. Residential segregation persists at high levels. "What is more," wrote Stephen Meyer in his 2000 book, *As Long as They Don't Move Next Door,* "many Americans of both races have come to accept racial separation as appropriate." Indeed, many whites see residential segregation as *desirable*. Across America, such elite sundown suburbs[37] as Darien, Connecticut; Naperville, Illinois; and Edina, Minnesota, are sought-after addresses, partly owing to, rather than despite, their racial makeup.[38]

Therefore this book has important implications for current racial policies. Most attempts to understand or ameliorate America's astounding residential concentrations of African Americans and Latinos have focused on the ghetto, barrio, or "changing neighborhood." We shall see, however, that these problem areas result primarily from exclusion elsewhere in the social system—from sundown towns and suburbs. But despite their causal importance, these white "ghettoes" have been dramatically underresearched. As a result, few Americans realize that metropolitan areas are not "naturally" segregated and that suburban whiteness has been produced by unsavory policies that continue in part to this day. If Americans understood the origins of overwhelmingly white communities, they might see that such neighborhoods are nothing to be proud of.

On the contrary, all this residential exclusion is bad for our nation. In fact, residential segregation is one reason race continues to be such a problem in America. But race really isn't the problem. Exclusion is the problem. The ghetto—with all its pathologies—isn't the problem; the elite sundown suburb—seemingly devoid of social difficulties—is the problem. As soon as we realize that the problem in America is white supremacy, rather than black existence or black inferiority, then it becomes clear that sundown towns and suburbs are an intensification of the problem, not a solution to it. So long as racial inequality is encoded in the most basic single fact in our society—where one can live—the United States will face continuing racial tension, if not overt conflict.

Thus the continued existence of overwhelmingly white communities is terribly important. Moreover, residential segregation exacerbates all other forms of racial discrimination. Segregated neighborhoods make it easier to discriminate against African Americans in schooling, housing, and city services, for instance. We shall see that residential segregation also causes employment inequalities by isolating African Americans from the social networks where job openings are discussed. Thus some of the inadequacies for which white Americans blame black Americans are products of, rather than excuses for, residential segregation.

All-white communities also make it easier for their residents to think badly of nonwhites. Because so many whites live in sundown neighborhoods, their stereotypes about how African Americans live remain intact, unchallenged by contact with actual black families living day-to-day lives. In fact, these stereotypes get intensified because they help rationalize living in sundown neighborhoods in the first place. Black stereotypes about whites also go unchallenged by experience. Trying to teach second-graders not to be prejudiced is an uphill battle in an all-white primary school in a culture that values all-white communities. Among adults, living in overwhelmingly white neighborhoods and suburbs ties in with opposing policies that might decrease the sharp differences between the life chances of blacks and whites in our society.

The Plan of the Book

This book is divided into six parts. Part I, "Introduction," consists of this chapter, "The Importance of Sundown Towns," and Chapter 2, "The Nadir: Incubator of Sundown Towns." Chapter 2 begins with the "springtime of race relations" following the Civil War, when blacks moved everywhere in America. Then it tells of the time when race relations actually moved backward—the era that not only gave rise to sundown towns, but made them seem necessary, at least to some white Americans. Today's overwhelmingly white towns, suburbs, and neighborhoods linger as living legacies from that tragic period when race relations grew harsher.

Part II, "The History of Sundown Towns," includes three chapters. Chapter 3, "The Great Retreat," suggests a term for the massive strategic withdrawal that African Americans—and Chinese Americans before them—were forced to make from northern and western towns and rural areas to our large cities. Until now, historians have largely overlooked the forced departure of minorities, the Nadir period in the North that gave rise to the Great Retreat, and the "springtime of race relations" in the North that preceded the Nadir. "The Great Retreat" also shows statistically how widespread the sundown town movement was. Chapter 4, "How Sundown Towns Were Created," explains the mechanisms underlying these statistics. It supplies examples of the use of violence, threats, law, and official policy; informal means such as freeze-outs and buyouts; and suburban methods including zoning and public planning, all in the service of creating all-white communities. Chapter 5, "Sundown Suburbs," notes that the rush to the suburbs wasn't originally racial but became racially tagged after about 1900. Sundown suburbs then grew even more widespread than independent sundown towns and persisted in forming into the late 1960s. By the time the federal government finally switched sides and tried to undo the resulting segregation, great damage had been done to our metropolitan areas.

Part III, "The Sociology of Sundown Towns," also contains three chapters. Often a sundown town is located near an interracial town. What explains why the first went sundown while the second did not? What explains Anna-Jonesboro, for example, when five miles north, Cobden, Illinois, always allowed African Americans to live in it? Chapter 6, "Underlying Causes," suggests several basic conditions that underlie and predict sundown towns; unaware of these factors, many residents believe nonsensical or tautological "reasons." Chapter 7, "Catalysts and Origin Myths," deconstructs the triggering incidents that residents often invoke to justify their town's policy and shows how these stories function as origin myths. Chapter 8, "Hidden in Plain View: Knowing and Not Knowing About Sundown Towns," tells why most Americans have no idea that sundown towns exist. This chapter also sets forth the methods and evidence underlying the claims made throughout the book. Some readers suggested relegating this material to an appendix, but I need you to read the book actively, assessing my claims as you go along. I invite skeptics (which I hope includes all readers) to turn to this chapter at any point, and also to the "Portfolio" in the center of the book—photographs and newspaper headlines that introduce visually some of the evidence for these claims.

The two chapters of Part IV, "Sundown Towns in Operation," explain how, once they made their decision to go all-white, sundown communities managed to stay so white for so long. Chapter 9, "Enforcement," tells the sometimes heartbreaking consequences inflicted upon casual and even inadvertent visitors caught after dark in sundown towns, and the still worse repercussions that awaited persons of color who tried to move in permanently. Chapter 10, "Exceptions to the Sundown Rule," explains that many all-white towns allowed an exceptional African American or Chinese American or two to stay, even as they defined their communities as sundown towns. Usually these exceptions reinforced the sundown rule by making it all the more obvious.

Part V, "Effects of Sundown Towns" answers the question, what difference do these towns make? Its three chapters show that they have bad effects "On Whites" (Chapter 11), "On Blacks" (Chapter 12), and "On the Social System" (Chapter 13). The resulting pattern of "chocolate cites and vanilla suburbs" has damaged everything from Republican Party platforms to black employability and morale.

Part VI, "The Present and Future of Sundown Towns," contains two chapters. Chapter 14, "Sundown Towns Today," tells that many communities relaxed their prohibitions since about 1980, while others did not. This recent improvement has made choosing the appropriate verb tense difficult. Putting a practice in the past—"Fans in many sundown towns seemed affronted that African Americans dared to play in their town"—would mislead, because fans in many sundown towns continue to taunt visiting interracial athletic teams. At the same time, writing "such elite sundown suburbs as Darien, Connecticut" might imply that Darien still keeps blacks out today—which I don't know and even doubt. I resolved my verb tense dilemma as best I could, usually using the continuing past ("has excluded") or the present tense ("keeps out") if a town kept out African Americans (or other groups) for decades, regardless of whether it does so now.[39] *Such statements do not necessarily mean that the town is sundown to this day.* Please do not assume that a town still keeps out African Americans without checking it out yourself. Meanwhile, concurrent with this improvement, Americans have also been developing new forms of exclusion, based no longer on race—at least not explicitly—but on differences in social class that then get reified on the landscape in the form of gated communities.

The final chapter is titled "The Remedy: Integrated Neighborhoods and Towns." It suggests tactics for everyone from members of Congress to individual homeowners who want to end sundown towns—surely a national disgrace.

The Penultimate Denial of Human Rights

How could America do these things? How could white Americans drive Chinese Americans and African Americans and sometimes other groups from hundreds of towns? How could thousands of other towns and suburbs flatly prevent African Americans, Jewish Americans, or others from living in them? After all, after life itself, allowing someone to live in a place is perhaps the most basic human right of all. If people cannot live in a town, they cannot attend school in it, vote, or participate in any other form of civic life or human interaction.

In the 1857 *Dred Scott* decision, that most racist of all Supreme Court decrees, Chief Justice Roger B. Taney held that African Americans "had for more than a century before been regarded as beings of an inferior order, and altogether unfit to associate with the white race, either in social or political relations, and so far inferior, that they had no rights which the white man was bound to respect." Between 1890 and the 1930s—and continuing to the present in some places—many white Americans actually tried to put his words into practice, in the form of sundown towns and suburbs. "After all," they reasoned, "if the founding fathers and their successors, including Taney, thought

African Americans were 'altogether unfit to associate with the white race,' then let's stop associating with them. And let's do this, not by altering *our* behavior, but by limiting *their* choices—by excluding *them*."

Of course, other countries have flatly denied the rights of an entire race of people to live in a town or wider area. In Germany, beginning in 1934, according to historian James Pool, local Nazis began to put up signs "outside many German towns and villages: JEWS NOT WANTED HERE." Pool goes on:

> Before long the signs outside some towns were worded in more threatening terms: JEWS ENTER THIS TOWN AT YOUR OWN RISK. At this point the Nazi government in Berlin reluctantly intervened. . . . Although Berlin ordered all threatening signs removed, most of them stayed up.

Two years later, most German sundown signs actually came down at Berlin's insistence as Germany prepared for the 1936 Olympic Games. During this period, hundreds and perhaps thousands of towns in America already displayed signs like the ones the Germans were putting up, directed against African Americans, but our government in Washington never ordered any of them removed, not even those on California highways as America prepared for the 1932 Los Angeles Olympics. To be sure, beginning in 1938, Germany's "Final Solution" made communities free of Jews in a much more vicious way than anything the United States ever achieved. Still, it is sobering to realize that many jurisdictions in America had accomplished by 1934–36 what Nazis in those years could only envy.[40]

Residential Segregation Lives On

Germany reversed course in 1945. The Allies forced it to. The sundown town movement in the United States did not begin to slow until 1968, however, even cresting in about 1970, and we cannot yet consign sundown towns to the past. More than half a century after the U.S. Supreme Court decreed in *Brown v. Board of Education* that whites cannot keep blacks out of white schools, and more than forty years after the 1964 Civil Rights Act made it illegal to keep them out of a restaurant, hundreds of towns and suburbs still keep African Americans out of entire municipalities.

Several towns near Colp, Illinois, for example, are *not* done with being sundown towns. Consider the town with which we began this chapter, Anna, some 30 miles southwest. In September 2002, to the best knowledge of

Anna's reference librarian and newspaper editor, neither Anna nor its companion city of Jonesboro had a single African American household within their corporate limits. In 2004, a rural resident of the Anna-Jonesboro School District confirmed, "Oh no, there are no black people in Anna today." Do these towns still actively keep out African Americans, or is their all-white nature merely the result of inertia and reputation? At the very least, Anna and Jonesboro—like most other sundown towns—have taken no public steps to announce any change in policy.[41]

Anna is only an example, of course. Hundreds of other towns and suburbs across the United States have kept out African Americans even longer than Anna and are equally white today. Unfortunately for our country, America has not reached the point where all-white towns and suburbs are seen as anachronisms. Indeed, in a way, sundown towns are still being created. White families are still moving to overwhelmingly if not formally all-white exurbs distant from inner suburbs that have now gone interracial. And Americans of all races are moving to gated communities, segregated on income lines and sometimes informally segregated on racial grounds as well.

Not only our sundown past but also our sundown present affronts me. I believe that Americans who understand that all-white towns still exist—partly owing to past government actions and inactions—will share my anger and will support government and private actions in the opposite direction, to open them to everyone. I hope also that lifting the veil of secrecy that conceals the overt and often violent cleansings that produced sundown towns and suburbs will prompt Americans to see these "racially pure" communities as places to be avoided rather than desired.

Where we live does affect how we think, and eliminating all-white towns and neighborhoods will decrease racial prejudice and misunderstanding. Social psychologists have long found that a good way to reduce prejudice is for different people to live together and interact on an equal footing. We will see in "The Remedy" that racial integration usually does work. It helps to humanize most individuals who live in interracial communities, and the existence of such communities helps to humanize our culture as a whole. As sociologist Robert Park wrote decades ago, "Most if not all cultural changes in society will be correlated with changes in territorial organization, and every change in the territorial and occupational distribution of the population will effect changes in the existing culture." So if we want American culture to be nonracist, Park would tell us, we have to eradicate our racially exclusive communities.[42]

"The Remedy" will challenge you to do something about the history it presents. I am optimistic: at last, many people seem ready to talk about sundown towns, ready even to change them. Americans have come to decry overt racism, after all, and the task could hardly be more important. Indeed, integrating sundown towns and suburbs becomes, ultimately, a battle for our nation's soul, and for its future.

To summarize, waves of ethnic cleansing swept across the United States between about 1890 and 1940, leaving thousands of sundown towns in their wake. Thousands of sundown suburbs formed even later, some as late as the 1960s. As recently as the 1970s, elite suburbs like Edina, Minnesota, would openly turn away Jewish and black would-be home buyers. Some towns and suburbs were still sundown when this book went to press in 2005.

At this point you may be shocked: how could it happen that in 1909 whites in Anna, Illinois, might run every African American resident out of their community, never to return? That many other towns across the United States could take similar actions as late as 1954? That Hawthorne, California, had a sign at its city limits in the 1930s that said, "Nigger, Don't Let The Sun Set On YOU In Hawthorne"? Or that Minden and Gardnerville, Nevada, sounded a whistle at 6 PM to tell all American Indians to get out of town before sundown?[43]

To understand how so many sundown towns formed in the United States, we must examine the era—1890 to 1940—that gave rise to them.

2

The Nadir: Incubator of Sundown Towns

The elevation of the Negro race from slavery to the full rights of citizenship is the most important political change we have known since the adoption of the Constitution of 1787. No thoughtful man can fail to appreciate its beneficent effect upon our institutions and people. . . . The influence of this force will grow greater and bear richer fruit with the coming years. . . .

The emancipated race has already made remarkable progress. . . . So far as my authority can lawfully extend they shall enjoy the full and equal protection of the Constitution and the laws.
—President James A. Garfield, Inaugural Address, 1881

In the half decade of the 1860s following the Civil War and during the 1870s, the organized activities and individual happenings within the Negro group still found a place in the newspapers, but as the emotions of the Civil War era cooled and Negroes gradually took their place in the everyday life of Northern communities, the special interest and the ready sympathy of earlier days waned.
—Leola Bergmann, after analyzing Iowa newspapers[1]

THE FACTS ABOUT SUNDOWN TOWNS prove hard for many people to believe, partly because high school textbooks in American history present a nation that has always been getting better, in everything from methods of transportation to race relations. We used to have slavery; now we don't. We used to have lynchings; now we don't. Baseball used to be all-white; now it isn't. Step by step, race relations have somehow improved on their own, according to the textbooks' archetypal story line of constant progress, and the whole problem has now been fixed or is on the way to being fixed. "The U.S. has done more than any other nation in history to provide equal rights for all," *The American Tradition,* a representative textbook, blandly assures us, as if its authors have examined race relations in Andorra, Botswana, Canada, or any other country.[2]

The assumption of progress has blinded us to the possibility that sometimes things grew worse. As a result, most Americans have no idea that race relations *deteriorated* in the 1890s and in the first third of the twentieth century. Sundown towns cannot be understood outside of the historical period that spawned them. This era, from 1890 to the 1930s, when African Americans were forced back into noncitizenship, is called the Nadir of race relations in the United States.

Unfortunately, most Americans do not even know the term. Instead, the period has been broken up into several eras, most of them inaccurate as well as inconsequential, such as "Gay Nineties" or "Roaring Twenties." During the Gay Nineties, for example, the United States suffered its second-worst depression ever, as well as the Pullman and Homestead strikes and other major labor disputes. Thus "Gay Nineties" hardly signifies more than the decade itself and leads logically to the query, "Gay for whom?"

Historian Rayford Logan began to establish "Nadir of race relations" as a term in his 1954 book, *The Negro in American Life and Thought: The Nadir.* Since then, the idea that race relations actually grew worse has become well accepted in American history, but the deterioration has hitherto mainly been identified only in the South.[3]

Impact of the Civil War

To be sure, the idea of keeping out African Americans was not born in this period. It first occurred to northern whites during the slavery period. Before the Civil War, several entire states passed laws to accomplish this end. The 1848 Illinois state constitution provided:

> The General Assembly shall at its first session under the amended constitution
> pass such laws as will effectually prohibit free persons of color from immigrating
> to and settling in this state, and to effectually prevent the owners of slaves from
> bringing them into this state, for the purpose of setting them free.

Ohio, Michigan, Indiana, California, and Oregon passed similar laws, thus becoming "sundown states" so far as any new African Americans were concerned, although only Oregon's law saw much enforcement. No state made a serious effort to expel African Americans[4] already residing within its borders.

Until at least 1861, North and South, most white Americans defined "black inferiority" as the problem, to which slavery was the solution. The Civil War changed all that, at least for a time. As the war continued, on the United States side it became not just a struggle to maintain national unity, but also a war to end slavery. As early as 1862, U.S. soldiers were marching to songs such as George Root's "Battle Cry of Freedom":

> We will welcome to our numbers the loyal true and brave,
> Shouting the battle cry of freedom.
> And although he may be poor, not a man shall be a slave,
> Shouting the battle cry of freedom.[5]

During the war, many white U.S. soldiers met and came to know African Americans for the first time. The actions of these African Americans played a big role in challenging white racism. Slaves fled to Union lines to be free, to get married and launch normal family lives, to make a living, and to help the United States win the war. The contributions of black soldiers and sailors to the war effort made it harder for whites to deny that African Americans were fully human, since they were acting it. Real friendships formed—between white officers of United States Colored Troops and their men, between white officers in white units and their black orderlies, and between escaped Union POWs and the African Americans who sheltered them behind enemy lines. Ordinary enlisted men, white and black, came increasingly to rely on each other, albeit in separate units, for the mutual support necessary for survival on the battlefield.

Anti-racist Idealism During and After the Civil War

Thus it came to pass that during the Civil War and Reconstruction, especially in the North, most whites defined slavery as the problem, to which fuller civil rights for African Americans, exemplified in the Thirteenth, Fourteenth, and Fifteenth Amendments, would be the answer. As a result, for a time right after the war, anti-racist idealism played a dominant role in American political life. During this time, northern Republicans reinterpreted the Declaration of Independence to include African Americans among the "all men created equal," a process begun by Lincoln at Gettysburg. According to historians Shepherd McKinley and Heather Richardson, "Northern Republicans in 1865 had little doubt that upon setting the slaves free in southern society, they would overcome all temporary barriers, . . . accumulate capital, and achieve self-sufficiency." Congress passed important civil rights acts protecting black rights, and especially during U.S. Grant's first term (1869–73), the federal government even tried to enforce them. Consequently, African Americans lived under *better* conditions between 1865 and 1890—and not just in the South—than they would in the sad decades after 1890.[6]

After the Civil War, it was in Republicans' political interest to demand the right to vote for African American men, and the GOP led the nation to pass the Fifteenth Amendment to the Constitution, granting African Americans this vital prerogative of citizenship. Suffrage without regard to race was not just in Republicans' interest, however, but also in the national interest: black votes were needed in southern states to elect public officials who would support the United States rather than try to revive secession. Moreover, Republicans did not support rights for African Americans solely to advance their party. They also did so because they believed it was just. In Iowa, for example, before the Fifteenth Amendment passed nationally, Republicans thrice brought before the people a proposal to allow African Americans to vote. Although it took three tries, it finally passed. Republicans hardly did this for political gain; it enfranchised fewer than a thousand African Americans. They did it not to garner those few votes, but because it was the right thing to do.[7]

The Fourteenth Amendment, passed in 1868, also shows this anti-racist idealism. Often called the "equal rights amendment," this shining jewel of our Constitution conferred citizenship on all Americans, including state citizenship, and guaranteed every person, including African Americans, "due process" and "the equal protection of the laws."[8] Although the Thirteenth, Fourteenth, and Fifteenth amendments are called the "Reconstruction amendments," they also had important implications for the North, which, not having seceded, never underwent political reconstruction. The Fourteenth Amendment made moot the prewar state laws keeping out African Americans. The Fifteenth enfranchised African Americans, which only a handful of northern states had done prior to its passage.

In 1866 and 1868, white voters returned "radical" Republicans to Congress in landslides across the North that signaled their satisfaction with this anti-racist national policy. Republicans also won control of most northern state governments, even briefly of Maryland, formerly a slave state.

Welcoming African Americans, 1862–1890

Many towns and counties throughout the North reflected this anti-racism by welcoming African American immigrants during and after the Civil War. Often veterans played a direct role. For example, the Reverend J. B. Rogers from Fond du Lac, Wisconsin, chaplain of the 14th Wisconsin Volunteers, got reassigned to Cairo, Illinois, which had become a place of refuge for hundreds of African Americans dispossessed by the fighting farther south along the Mississippi River. Rogers set up a school and taught more than 400 ex-slaves. He then helped bring a group of his students, all former slaves, to Wisconsin. Sally Albertz, Fond du Lac historian, pictures the scene that October day in 1862:

> As a great crowd of people congregated at the train depot, a "car-load" of ex-slaves arrived at the Fond du Lac depot, chaperoned by Rev. Rogers. Word had spread throughout the area that anyone who wanted to "engage a contraband" or to help in any way should be at the depot. After the excitement had died down, local women served the weary travelers a welcome meal. They were then given rooms at the American Hotel until they could be hired out.

Whites in most Republican areas showed similar anti-racist behavior, and returning veterans brought African Americans whom they had met during the war home with them to many parts of the North.[9]

To be sure, anti-racism was hardly the sole response to the Civil War. Before the war, Democratic Party rhetoric had already been overtly racist to justify slavery. After the rise of the Republicans in the late 1850s, Democrats turned on the Republicans as the "party of miscegenation," a term for interracial sexual relations coined by Democrats in 1863. As the war continued, antiwar Democrats increasingly blamed "the Negro" for the conflict. Some Democratic towns in the North responded to their party's rhetoric, and to the frustrations generated by the long and bloody conflict, with a wave of forced expulsions of African Americans. Chesterton, Indiana, near Lake Michigan, drove out its African Americans in about 1863. That same year, a mob of twenty-five men led by an Anna, Illinois, doctor forced forty African American Civil War refugees, employed as farmworkers, to flee Union County. Also in 1863, white residents of Mason County forced out five African American residents; the county remained forcibly all-white for more than a century. The next chapter tells of an incident in 1864 in which LaSalle residents drove out a group of African Americans passing through that town en route to enlisting in the army. Since LaSalle lies in northern Illinois, Mason County in central Illinois, and Union County in southern Illinois, expelling African Americans during the Civil War was obviously widespread,[10] albeit mostly in Democratic areas.[11]

Nevertheless, in Republican communities, in the period 1865–90, letting in African Americans was seen to be the appropriate, even patriotic thing to do. It was in tune with the times. Many Americans really were trying to give our nation "a new birth of freedom"—freedom for African Americans—for which, as Lincoln had suggested, Union soldiers had died at Gettysburg.[12] Opening one's community to black families after the Civil War seemed right— like opening one's college campus to black students after the Civil Rights Movement a century later. Congress said so: the 1866 Civil Rights Act declared that "citizens of every race and color . . . shall have the same right . . . to inherit, purchase, lease, sell, hold, and convey real and personal property." Presidents said so—James A. Garfield at his inauguration in 1881, quoted at the head of the chapter, clearly stated that the nation had granted equal rights to African Americans and that this was fitting and proper. Quakers in particular, abolitionists before the war, now made it their business to welcome African Americans to their communities, hire them as farmworkers, blacksmiths, or domestics, and help them get a start. So did Unitarians, Congregationalists, and some Methodists and Presbyterians. We can see the result in census figures, summarized in Table 1 in the next chapter (page 56): African Americans went everywhere after the Civil War. By 1890, all across the North—in northeast Pennsylvania river valleys, in every Indiana county save one, deep in the north woods of Wisconsin, in every county of Montana and California—African Americans were living and working.

Historians have long recognized the importance of this era called Reconstruction, but they have usually confined their analysis of it to the South. Legally, Reconstruction did apply only to the South. But Reconstruction was also an ideological movement, and the ideological currents that motivated Reconstruction not only touched but emanated from the North. Historian Lerone Bennett called it "the first and, in many ways, the last real attempt to establish an interracial democracy in America." But most historians have not included the increased acceptance of African Americans across the towns and counties of the North as part of our national narrative. Reconstruction was a period of possibility for African Americans in the North, as in the South.[13]

Northern communities, especially where Republicans were in the majority, enjoyed something of a "springtime of race relations" between 1865 and 1890. During those years, African Americans voted, served in Congress, received some spoils from the Republican Party, worked as barbers, railroad firemen, midwives, mail carriers, and landowning farmers, and played other fully human roles in American society. Their new rights made African Americans optimistic, even buoyant. "Tell them we is risin'!" one ex-slave said to a northern writer, come to see for himself how the races were getting along in

the postwar South. The same confidence fueled the black dispersal throughout the postwar North.

The "Fusion" Period, 1877–1890

Supporters of white supremacy did not fold their tents and depart, however.
With increasing tenacity and Ku Klux Klan violence, Democrats fought the
interracial Republican coalitions for control of each southern state.[14] In
Louisiana, for example, in the summer and fall of 1868, white Democrats
killed more than a thousand people, mostly African Americans and white Republicans. The intimidation continued for eight more years, until by the beginning of 1877, the Democrats had more or less won control across the
South. But their victory was incomplete. African Americans still voted—
though not freely. Democrats set up "Fusion" tickets, giving blacks some
minor offices while Democrats won the governorships and dominated state
legislatures. But Democrats were never sure they could keep control of southern state governments against possible coalitions of African American voters
and white Republicans, Readjusters (William Mahone's party in Virginia),
and Populists. In Virginia, North Carolina, and Alabama, interracial coalitions briefly won statewide and would have won more often had elections
been fair. African Americans still had the rights of citizenship—at least formally—until the 1890s.

In the North, the impulse to grant blacks rights and welcome them did
not die with the end of Reconstruction either. Ironically, this is demonstrated
by Waverly, Ohio, noted in Chapter 1 as one of the few towns in America to be
sundown from its inception, before the Civil War. Waverly's treatment in the
massive 1884 *History of Lower Scioto Valley* includes this optimistic predic-
tion:

> Although the traditions of hostility toward his race keeps alive the fears of the
> black man, yet with the new order of things the people here, as elsewhere, have
> changed in their prejudices and it is altogether probable that now a Negro could
> take up his residence here in perfect freedom.[15]

Unfortunately, "the new order of things" was destined to last only six
more years. In 1890, trying to get the federal government to intervene against
violence and fraud in southern elections, the Republican senator from Massachusetts, Henry Cabot Lodge, introduced his Federal Elections Bill. It lost by
just one vote in the Senate. After its defeat, when Democrats again tarred Re-

publicans as "nigger lovers," now the Republicans replied in a new way. Instead of assailing Democrats for denying equal rights to African Americans, they backed away from the subject. The Democrats had worn them down. Thus the springtime of race relations during Reconstruction was short, and it was followed not by summer blooms but by the Nadir winter, and not just in the South but throughout the country. In Ohio, Waverly remained all-white for another century and boasted a sundown sign until after World War II.[16]

The "Three I's"

What caused this collapse? From the formation of the Republican Party in the mid-1850s through 1890, anti-racism had constituted its clearest point of difference vis-à-vis the Democrats. Now this contrast faded. The idealism spawned by the Civil War was fading too, as memories of the war dimmed. By 1890, only one American in three was old enough to have been alive when it ended; a still smaller proportion was old enough to have any memory of the war.[17] Millions more immigrated to the United States long after the war's end and played no role in it.

The ideology of anti-racism was further strained by three developments—"the three i's"—having nothing directly to do with black rights. The first was Indian wars. Although the federal government had guaranteed the Plains Indians their land "forever," after whites discovered gold in Colorado, the Dakotas, and elsewhere, they took it anyway. In 1890, the army destroyed the last important vestige of Native American independence in the massacre at Wounded Knee, South Dakota. If it was OK to take Indians' land because they weren't white, wasn't it OK to deny rights to African Americans, who weren't white either?[18]

Second, immigrants remained a problem for Republicans. Irish, Italian, and Polish Americans persisted in voting Democratic, no matter how Republicans tried to win them over. Republican intolerance of alcohol and of Catholicism played a role. On the Democratic side, the new hyphenated Americans immediately learned that it was in their interest to be considered "whites," differentiated from "blacks," who were still at the bottom of the social hierarchy. In the West, white miners and fishermen were competing with Chinese immigrants and hating them for it, and Democratic politicians shouted, "The Chinese must go!" In the East, the Democrats' continued white racism appealed to new European immigrants in competition with African Americans for jobs at the wharves, in the kitchens, on the railroads, and in the mines. Perhaps Republicans converted to a more racist position to win white ethnic votes. Or perhaps their anti-immigrant thinking, manifesting itself in jokes, slurs, and anti-immigrant cartoons, spilled over into increased racism vis-à-vis African Americans. Senator Lodge, who had pushed for black rights in 1890, helped found the Immigration Restriction League a few years later, to keep out "inferior" racial strains. How can a party claim to be basically superior to immigrants and still maintain "that all men are created equal"?[19]

Imperialism was the third *i*. The growing clamor to annex Hawaii included the claim that we could govern those brown people better than they could govern themselves. After winning the Spanish-American War, the McKinley administration used the same rationale to defend making war upon our allies, the Filipinos. Imperialism as an ideological fad was sweeping the West, and it both depended upon and in turn reinforced the ideology of white supremacy. After 1890, imperialism led the United States successively to dominate Hawaii, Puerto Rico, Cuba, the Philippines, Nicaragua, Haiti, the Dominican Republic, the Virgin Islands, and several other Caribbean and Central American nations. Democrats pointed out the inconsistency of denying real self-government to Hawaiians, Filipinos, Haitians, and others, partly on the basis of their alleged racial inferiority, while insisting on equal rights for African Americans. The Republicans had no real answer.

There were still other causes of the decline of Republican anti-racism. During what some historians call the Gilded Age, some capitalists amassed huge fortunes. Doing likewise became the dream of many Republicans, a goal that was hard to reconcile with the party's former talk of social justice.[20] This increasing stratification sapped America's historic belief that "all men are created equal." To justify the quest for wealth, a substitute ideology was created, Social Darwinism—the notion that the fittest rise to the top in society. It provided a potent rationale not only for class privilege, but for racial superiority as well.

The worsening of race relations cannot be explained by downturns such as the Panic of 1893, for the Nadir began before 1893 and persisted through economic ups and downs. To be sure, economic determinism and racial competition, usually exploited by the Democrats, played a part, as we have seen. But the deepening racism of the Nadir was first and foremost a cultural movement, stemming from the decay of Civil War idealism, the evolution of ideas such as imperialism and eugenics, changes in the Republican Party, and other historical developments. Therefore it was historically contingent, not preordained. *If* President Grant and his successors had achieved a fairer Indian policy, *if* the Senate had passed the Federal Elections Bill, *if* Republicans had not caved in on race after the bill's defeat, *if* McKinley had not attacked the

Philippines and taken us down the road to imperialism, *if* the national government had put down the white violence that ended the last interracial southern political movements between 1890 and 1898, *if* affluent WASPs had rejected instead of embraced the anti-Semitism that flourished around 1900—if any of these had happened, then the Nadir might never have occurred. Then if a town or suburb had tried to drive out or keep out African Americans in 1895 or 1909 or 1954, the federal government under the Fourteenth Amendment might have intervened. So might state governments have done.

Of course, ultimately racial superiority as an ideology derives from slavery. An Arkansas librarian whom I interviewed while doing research for this book put this as succinctly as I've heard it: "African Americans were the people enslaved. So whites had to make them intellectually inferior to justify enslaving them." Because there was slavery, blacks were stigmatized as a race and black skin became a badge of slavery. Because there was slavery, whites made African Americans a pariah people whose avoidance—except on unequal terms—conferred status upon whites. Thus because there was slavery, there was segregation. Ultimately, racism is a vestige of "slavery unwilling to die," as Supreme Court Justice William O. Douglas famously put it in 1968. In the final analysis, the Nadir period, as well as the sundown towns and suburbs it spawned, are relics of slavery. Like the Civil War itself, neither the Nadir nor sundown towns would have occurred absent slavery.[21]

The Nadir of Race Relations Sets In

We have seen that the Republicans removed themselves as an effective antiracist force after about 1891. The Democrats already called themselves "the white man's party." It followed that African Americans played no significant role in either political party from 1892 on. Now, regardless of which party controlled it, the federal government stood by idly as white southerners used terror, fraud, and "legal" means to eliminate African American voters. Mississippi pioneered the "legal" means in 1890 when it passed a new state constitution that made it impossible for most black Mississippians to vote or hold public office. All other southern and border states emulated Mississippi by 1907.

In 1894, Democrats in Congress repealed the remaining federal election statutes. Now the Fifteenth Amendment was lifeless, for it had no extant laws to enforce it. In 1896, in *Plessy v. Ferguson,* the United States Supreme Court declared de jure (by law) racial segregation legal, which caused it to spread in at least twelve northern states.[22] In 1898, Democrats rioted in Wilmington,

North Carolina, driving out the mayor and all other Republican officeholders and killing at least twelve African Americans. The McKinley administration did nothing, allowing this coup d'état to stand. Congress became resegregated in 1901 when Congressman George H. White of North Carolina failed to win reelection owing to the disfranchisement of black voters in his state. No African American served in Congress again until 1929, and none from the South until 1973.

Southern whites, at least Confederate and neo-Confederate whites, were delighted. Indeed, in about 1890, the South, or rather the white neo-Confederate South, finally won the Civil War. That is, the Confederacy's "great truth"—quoting Alexander Stephens, vice president of the Confederacy, speaking on March 21, 1861: "Our new government's foundations are laid, its cornerstone rests, upon the great truth that the Negro is not equal to the white man"—became national policy. States as far north as North Dakota passed new laws outlawing interracial marriage. Lynchings rose to their all-time peak, and not just in the South. A lynching is a public murder, not necessarily of an African American, although four of every five lynching victims have been nonwhites. The public nature of a lynching signaled that the dominant forces in the community were in league with the perpetrators. Portfolio 5 shows the further development of the "spectacle lynching," publicized ahead of time, that drew crowds in the hundreds, even thousands. White Americans, north and south, joined hands to restrict African Americans' civil and economic rights.[23]

After 1890, as in the South, Jim Crow practices tightened throughout the North. The so-called Progressive movement was for whites only; often its "reforms" removed the last local black leaders from northern city councils in favor of commissioners elected citywide. Northern whites attacked African Americans, verbally and often literally. Segregation swept through public accommodations. In 1908, the famous reporter Roy Stannard Baker toured the North for an article, "The Color Line in the North." He noted the deterioration even in Boston, the old citadel of abolitionism: "A few years ago no hotel or restaurant in Boston refused Negro guests; now several hotels, restaurants, and especially confectionery stores, will not serve Negroes, even the best of them." Writing of the day-to-day interactions of whites and blacks in the Midwest, Frank Quillen observed in 1913 that race prejudice "is increasing steadily, especially during the last twenty years." In the 1920s, Harvard barred an African American student from the very dormitory where his father had lived decades earlier when attending the university. *Like Reconstruction, the Nadir of race relations was national.*[24]

A 1912 referendum across President Garfield's home state of Ohio exemplified most dramatically America's grievous retraction of "the full rights of citizenship" for African Americans, about which he had rightly bragged in 1881. In 1912, even blacks' right to vote was questioned in Ohio, when voters rejected an amendment to the state constitution removing "white" from the clause defining eligibility for the franchise. In 1870, Ohio had ratified the Fifteenth Amendment, which granted African Americans the right to vote. Ever since the amendment became law in that year, black men had been voting in Ohio. Because federal law superseded state law, the 1912 action was only cosmetic, to bring the state constitution in line with the federal one. Yet by rejecting the change, white Ohioans in 1912 made clear that they wanted black voting to stop.[25]

Leola Bergmann carefully analyzed Iowa newspapers and found a shocking decrease in sympathy and increase in antipathy among whites in that state, which President Grant had called "bright radical star" after it granted African Americans the right to vote. In the quote at the head of the chapter, she tells of the inclusion of "the organized activities and individual happenings within the Negro group" in newspapers up to about 1880. Then such stories gradually stopped appearing. Worse, she noted, "in the kind of news that was reported one can detect the opposition that slowly accumulated in the public mind." Nearly all the stories about African Americans that newspapers printed in the late 1880s and throughout the 1890s concerned crime. "If colored groups engaged in worthwhile educative or social projects—and certainly they did—newspaper readers were not often apprised of it." Bergmann supplies an example—a black Iowan was named ambassador to Liberia in 1890—that went wholly unreported in the Iowa press.[26]

Occupationally, blacks fared even worse. Before the Nadir, African Americans worked as carpenters, masons, foundry and factory workers, postal carriers, and so on. After 1890, in both the North and the South, whites expelled them from these occupations. The expulsions were most glaring in sport, supposedly a meritocracy that rewards superior performance no matter who exhibits it. African Americans had played baseball in the major leagues in the 1880s. Whites forced out the last black at the beginning of the Nadir, in 1889; the last African Americans left the minor leagues in the 1890s. In 1911, the Kentucky Derby eliminated black jockeys. Only boxing offered a relief, but Jack Johnson's 1910 victory over Jim Jeffries, the Great White Hope, just confirmed whites' stereotype of African Americans as dangerous fighters.[27]

The *Chicago Defender,* a nationally important black newspaper, was full of articles between 1910 and 1925 chronicling the erosion of black employment. In 1911, an article headlined "The Passing of Colored Firemen in Chicago" lamented that only seven black firefighters were left, whites having forced out all the rest. Indeed, in some ways the North proceeded to treat African Americans *worse* than the South did. Ironically, segregation, which grew more entrenched in the South than in the North after the end of Reconstruction in 1877, created some limited opportunities for African American workers in Dixie. If the job was clearly defined as inferior, southern whites were happy to hire African Americans to cook their food, drive their coaches and later their cars, be their "yard boy," even nurse their babies. (The term *boy*, applied to adult male African Americans, itself implies less than a man.) Thus traditional white southerners rarely drove all African Americans out of their communities. Who would then do the dirty work? During and after slavery this pattern spread to the North, but only to a limited degree. Around 1900, many white Americans, especially outside the traditional South, grew so racist that they came to abhor contact with African Americans even when that contact expressed white supremacy. If African Americans were inferior, they reasoned, then why employ them? Why tolerate them at all?[28]

How the Nadir Gave Birth to a Sundown Town

Harrison, Arkansas, had been a reasonably peaceful interracial town in the early 1890s. "The town had its colored section in those days," in the words of Boone County historian Ralph Rea. "There was never a large Negro population in Harrison, probably never more than three or four hundred, but they had their church, their social life, and in the main there was little friction between them and the whites." Rea goes on to tell how whites and African Americans patronized a black barbecue to help fund a school for African American children. While the whites already *had* a school, of course, funded by public tax monies, nevertheless the barbecue shows cordial social intercourse between the races. Then, throughout Arkansas as elsewhere, race relations worsened around the turn of the twentieth century. Democrat Jeff Davis (no relation to the Confederate president) successfully ran for governor in 1900, 1902, and 1904, and then for the U.S. Senate in 1906. His language grew more Negrophobic with each campaign. "We have come to a parting of the way with the Negro," he shouted. "If the brutal criminals of that race . . . lay unholy hands upon our fair daughters, nature is so riven and shocked that the dire compact produces a social cataclysm."[29]

Another factor was the bankruptcy on July 1, 1905, of the Missouri and North Arkansas Railroad, intended to connect Harrison with Eureka

Springs and ultimately St. Louis and the world. This put unemployed railroad track layers, some of them African American, on the streets of Harrison and was also an economic hardship for townspeople who had invested in the scheme. Then, according to Arkansas researchers Jacqueline Froelich and David Zimmermann, on Saturday night, September 30, 1905, "a black man, identified only as Dan, reportedly seeking shelter from the cold, was arrested for breaking into the Harrison residence of Dr. John J. Johnson and was jailed with another African-American prisoner, called Rabbit." Two days later, whites in Harrison took Davis's campaign rhetoric to heart. In Zimmermann's words:

> A white mob stormed the building and took these two Negroes from jail along with several others, to the country, where they were whipped and ordered to leave. The rioters swept through Harrison's black neighborhood with terrible intent. The mob of 20 or 30 men, armed with guns and clubs, reportedly tied men to trees and whipped them, tied men and women together and threw them in a 4-foot hole in Crooked Creek, burned several homes, and warned all Negroes to leave town that night, which most of them did without taking any of their belongings.

"From house to house in the colored section they went," conclude Froelich and Zimmermann, "sometimes threatening, sometimes using the lash, always issuing the order that hereafter, 'no Nigger had better let the sun go down on 'em.' "[30]

Three or four wealthy families sheltered their African American servants, who stayed on for a few more years. Then in 1909, another African American was charged with a crime—armed robbery, possibly also including rape—and had to be spirited out of town to avoid a lynch mob. "This mob proved the last straw for even the most resilient of the 1905 survivors," in Zimmermann's words. "Fearing for their lives, most of Harrison's [remaining] black residents fled town the night of January 28." Harrison remained a sundown town at least until 2002.[31]

African Americans, Not Racism, Become "the Problem"

Harrison exemplifies how the increasing racism of the Nadir led to the expulsion of African Americans. How were northern whites to explain to themselves their acquiescence in the white South's obliteration of the political and civil rights of African Americans in places such as Harrison? How could they defend their own increasing occupational and social discrimination against African Americans?

The easiest way would be to declare that African Americans had never deserved equal rights in the first place. After all, went this line of thought, conditions had significantly improved for African Americans. Slavery was over. Now a new generation of African Americans had come of age, never tainted by the "peculiar institution." Why were they still at the bottom? African Americans themselves must be the problem. *They* must not work hard enough, think as well, or have as much drive, compared to whites.[32] The Reconstruction amendments (Thirteenth, Fourteenth, and Fifteenth) provided African Americans with a roughly equal footing in America, most whites felt. If they were still at the bottom, it must be their own fault.[33]

Ironically, the worse the Nadir got, the more whites blamed blacks for it. The increasing segregation and exclusion led whites to demonize African Americans and their segregated enclaves. African Americans earned less money than whites, had lower standing in society, and no longer held public office or even voted in much of the nation. Again, no longer could this obvious inequality be laid at slavery's doorstep, for slavery had ended around 1865. Now "white Northerners came to view blacks as disaffected, lazy, and dangerous rabble," according to Heather Richardson. "By the 1890s, white Americans in the North concurred that not only was disfranchisement justified for the 'Un-American Negro,' but that he was by nature confined to a state of 'permanent semi-barbarism.' "[34]

To this day, public opinion polls show that many nonblack Americans— especially those who live in towns that have few African Americans whom they might get to know as individuals—still believe these generalizations, at least when they are phrased more politely. To be sure, the theme of African Americans as problems doesn't stand up to scrutiny. Whites forced out African American from major league baseball not because they couldn't play well, but because they could. Whites expelled black jockeys from the Kentucky Derby not because they were incompetent, but because they won 15 of the first 28 derbies. They drove blacks out of the job of postal carrier so they could do it themselves, not because blacks couldn't do it. The foregoing seems obvious, but when it comes to housing, even today, deep inside white culture as a legacy from the Nadir is the sneaking suspicion that African Americans *are* a problem, so it *is* best to keep them out.[35]

History, Popular Culture, and Science Legitimize the Nadir

During the Nadir, America took a wrong turn, North as well as South. In fact, we took perhaps the wrongest turn we have ever taken as a nation, a turn so wrong that we have not yet been able to comprehend all that it has done to us. In these years white Americans who never met an African American became racist anyway, because stereotypes of white superiority resonated throughout American culture. Historians played a major role. After the final overthrow of Reconstruction in 1890, historians converted the era into a tale of oppressed whites, beset by violence and corruption. As Harvard's Albert Bushnell Hart put it in 1905:

> Every [southern] legislature had Negro members, and some of them a Negro majority.[36] Most of these Negroes were ignorant men who were controlled by two classes of whites, called "scalawags" (southern Republicans) and "carpet-baggers" (northern men who had gone down South to get into politics). Taxes were increased, debts run up, and the extravagance and corruption of some of the legislatures surpass belief.

Such interpretations so distorted the historical record that by 1935 black scholar W. E. B. DuBois lamented, "We have got to the place where we cannot use our experiences during and after the Civil War for the uplift and enlightenment of mankind."[37] Even today, these interpretations from the Nadir still distort high school American history textbooks, including their portrayal of such men as John Brown and Ulysses Grant.[38]

During the Nadir, minstrel shows came to dominate our popular culture. They had been invented before the Civil War but flourished after 1890. In our electronic age, it is hard to imagine how prevalent minstrel shows became. "By the turn of the century," in the words of historian Joseph Boskin, "practically every city, town, and rural community had amateur minstrel groups." Minstrel shows both caused and reflected the Nadir. As black poet James Weldon Johnson put it, minstrel shows "fixed the tradition of the Negro as only an irresponsible, happy-go-lucky, wide-grinning, loud-laughing, shuffling, banjo-playing, singing, dancing sort of being." James De Vries, who studied Monroe, Michigan, in this era, wrote that minstrel shows portrayed African Americans as "the complete antithesis of all those qualities of character valued as important and worthwhile by white Americans." In small towns across the North, where few blacks existed to correct this impression, these stereotypes provided the bulk of white "knowledge" about what African Americans were like.[39]

In the twentieth century, movies gradually replaced minstrelsy and its offspring, vaudeville. Unfortunately for race relations, the first grand epic, *The Birth of a Nation,* released by D. W. Griffith in 1915, right in the heart of the Nadir, was perhaps the most racist major movie ever made. It lionized the first Ku Klux Klan (1865–75) as the savior of white southern civilization and fueled a nationwide Klan revival. Near the end of the Nadir, in 1936, *Gone with the Wind* sold a million hardbound books in its first month; the book and the resulting film, the highest-grossing movie of all time, further convinced whites that noncitizenship was appropriate for African Americans.[40]

Also in the new century, Social Darwinism morphed into eugenics, which provides the ultimate rationale for blaming the victim. Not only are the poor at the bottom owing to their own fault, they cannot even be helped, eugenics tells us, because the fault lies in their genes. Anthropologists measured average brain sizes of people around the world and concluded that whites' brains were larger. According to historian Richard Weiss, "Organized eugenics got its immediate impetus at a meeting of the American Breeders Association in 1904"—and we are not talking about dogs. In 1909, Harvard's president Charles W. Eliot, denounced "any mixture of racial stocks." He and Madison Grant agreed that white Anglo-Saxons deserved to be on top, but both worried that they might not stay there unless they took steps to keep other races out, which is why Grant wrote *The Passing of the Great Race* in 1916. Margaret Sanger, patron saint of birth control, was another stalwart believer in eugenics who admitted, "We do not want word to get out that we want to exterminate the Negro population." In the 1920s, the *Saturday Evening Post* began to quote and commend Grant's ideas. Grant, a stalwart in the American Breeders Association and trustee of the American Museum of Natural History, framed a bill restricting immigration that reached Congress in 1924.[41]

Anti-Semitism increased as well. During World War I, the U.S. Army for the first time considered Jews "a special problem whose loyalty to the US was open to question." Along with other government agencies (and the Ku Klux Klan), the Military Intelligence Department mounted a campaign against Jewish immigrants that helped convince Congress to pass Grant's restrictive immigration bill in 1924. In the 1920s and '30s, many state legislatures passed sterilization laws for people of "dubious stock." These people included isolated rural folk, interracial people, the poor, and those with low IQ test scores.[42]

IQ tests and the Scholastic Aptitude Test (SAT) came to the fore at this time, as the handmaidens of eugenic theory. In 1910, Henry Goddard began administering intelligence tests as indicators of fitness for citizenship to would-be immigrants at Ellis Island. Around that time Louis Terman modified Alfred Binet's IQ test into the Stanford-Binet IQ Test. Robert Yerkes developed the U.S. Army's "alpha test" and used it during World War I. Carl Brigham produced the SAT in the early 1920s. Each of these psychometricians believed that intelligence was innate, some races had more than others, and white Anglo-Saxons came out on top. Their tests "proved" as much— blacks, Jews, Slavs, and Italians did poorly. Brigham later underwent a dramatic but little-publicized change of heart, concluding that test scores mostly reflected social background and experience, but the damage had been done.

Other branches of social and biological science chimed in. E. A. Ross, president of the American Sociological Association, Henry F. Osborn, the paleontologist who named *Tyrannosaurus rex,* and zoologist Louis Agassiz claimed that their respective sciences proved that blacks were inferior. Physical anthropologists who believed that the "black race" evolved earlier than the "white race" concluded that blacks were therefore more primitive, while those who believed that blacks developed later than whites also concluded that blacks were more primitive, being "closer to the ape."[43]

The Nadir Continued to About 1940

From 1913 to 1921, Woodrow Wilson was president; he was surely the most racist president since Andrew Johnson. A southerner, Wilson was an outspoken white supremacist who used his power as chief executive to segregate the federal government. If blacks were doing the same tasks as whites, such as typing letters or sorting mail, they had to be fired or placed in separate rooms or at least behind screens. Wilson segregated the U.S. Navy, which had not previously been segregated; now blacks could only be cooks, firemen, and dishwashers at sea. He appointed southern whites to political offices previously held by African Americans. His legacy was extensive: he effectively closed the Democratic Party to African Americans for another two decades, and parts of the federal government stayed segregated into the 1950s and beyond.[44]

Triggered by the astounding success of *The Birth of a Nation,* the Ku Klux Klan rose again after 1915, only this time the Klan was national, not southern. It dominated state politics for a time in the 1920s in Oregon, Colorado, Oklahoma, Indiana, Georgia, and Maine, and had great influence throughout rural and small-town America. In some communities, especially towns that had already driven out their African Americans, the KKK targeted white ethnics, such as (Catholic) Italians, Poles, or Jews. Klan support was another reason why Congress passed and President Coolidge signed the 1924 immigration act to restrict newcomers from just about everywhere except northern and western Europe.

It's hard to date the end of this terrible era precisely. According to W. E. B. DuBois, "The election of 1928 probably represented the lowest point to which the influence of the Negro in politics ever fell in the United States since enfranchisement." He thus implies that politically at least, things got better after about 1930. The idea that whites had every right to bar nonwhites from "white" occupations and communities hardly died in 1930, however, and the Nadir hardly ended in that year.[45]

On the contrary, another group faced its own crisis in the 1930s, as the 1930 census reclassified Mexican Americans from white to nonwhite. This helped make the 1930s a mini-nadir for Chicano-Anglo relations. Several California towns followed up on the census reclassification by segregating Chicanos from Anglos in their public schools. During the Depression, the United States by official policy deported thousands of Mexican workers and their families, including many Mexican Americans, to Mexico. According to a survey of race relations across Colorado published by the University of Colorado Latino/a Research and Policy Center in 1999, "In 1936, a huge banner flew in [Greeley]: 'All Mexican and other aliens to leave the State of Colorado at once by order of Colorado State vigilantes.'"[46]

The Great Depression also intensified the pressure on African Americans. "Menial public service jobs such as street-cleaning and garbage collection, to which 'no self-respecting white man' would stoop a decade or so ago, are rapidly becoming exclusively white men's jobs," wrote sociologists Willis Weatherford and Charles S. Johnson in 1934. In some towns whites now drove blacks from the position of hotel waiter and porter. Black barbers (for whites) had been under attack for decades, and more barbers were forced out as the Depression set in. In 1929, white elevator operators replaced blacks in Jefferson City, Missouri, a setback that symbolized the difficulties African Americans faced throughout the country. After all, the position of elevator operator, while it has its ups and downs, is hardly a skilled or prestigious job. If whites could now deem blacks unfit for *that* job, what might be left for them? Certainly not the National Football League: the NFL, which had allowed black players and even a black coach in the 1920s, banned African Americans in 1933.[47]

The leadership of the new Congress of Industrial Organizations (CIO) unions in the 1930s did campaign against the exclusion of African Americans in the auto industry and some other manufacturing areas. Otherwise, as labor unions gained in power during the 1930s and into the '40s, the position of African Americans grew worse. In Missouri, according to *Missouri's Black Heritage,* "white labor unions, traditionally hostile to black workers, became even more so during the 1930s." Railroads had been the largest single employer of African Americans. To be sure, they had never hired blacks as locomotive engineers (by definition a "white job" requiring intelligence) but they had in some states as firemen (a "black job" involving shoveling coal into a hot firebox). Now unemployed whites shot at and killed black railroad firemen, making that a "white job" in many states. In 1932, white workers on just one railroad, the Illinois Central, killed ten African American trainmen in a campaign to drive them out of railroad jobs. By 1940, white unions had mostly thrown blacks out of all railroad work, except for Pullman porters, who supplied personal service to sleeping-car passengers.[48]

The administration of Franklin D. Roosevelt was largely under the thumb of white southerners so far as race relations was concerned, at least to 1938.[49] The president never pushed for an anti-lynching bill, even though such a bill would merely have criminalized a crime and although Republicans did try to pass it. Housing the government built or subsidized for defense workers during World War II was deliberately more segregated even than the housing in surrounding communities. Indeed, under FDR the federal government built seven new towns that explicitly kept out African Americans. The armed forces also maintained rigid segregation throughout the war.

FDR's economic programs were legally open to all Americans without regard to race, however, and they spoke to the poverty many African Americans endured during the Depression, even if they were not administered fairly. In 1941, Roosevelt also did set up the Fair Employment Practices Committee, which opened some defense plants to black workers. These policies, along with the symbolic gestures of Eleanor Roosevelt, the rise of the CIO, and processes set in motion by Adolf Hitler and his demise, led to some improvement in race relations beginning around 1940. That's why I now date the Nadir as 1890–1940.

Setting the Stage for the Great Retreat

Thus the textbook archetype of uninterrupted progress falsifies the history of race relations between 1890 and the 1930s. It is almost unimaginable how racist the United States became during the Nadir. If African Americans in those years had experienced only white indifference, rather than overt opposition—often legal and sometimes violent—they could have continued to win the Kentucky Derby, deliver mail, and buy homes in "white" towns and neighborhoods. The ideology of white supremacy increasingly pervaded American culture during this era, more even than during slavery. Convinced by this ideology that African Americans were inferior, whites all across America asked, "Why even let them live in our community?"

The next chapter tells the result: the "Great Retreat" of African Americans from towns and rural areas across the North to black ghettoes in large northern cities. We live with the results—sundown towns and suburbs—to this day. They form the most visible residue on the American landscape of the nightmare called the Nadir.

PART II

The History of
Sundown Towns

3

The Great Retreat

In spite of the fact that the total Negro population of Indiana showed a fivefold increase between 1860 and 1900, some parts of the state showed little or no increase, while there was actually a decline in some places. In some instances this was due to a deliberate anti-Negro policy. . . . Some communities gained a reputation for being so hostile that no Negro dared stay overnight in them.
—Emma Lou Thornbrough, *The Negro in Indiana,* 1957[1]

DURING THE NADIR, deliberate policies, formal and informal, created America's most complete form of residential segregation: the complete exclusion of African Americans—and sometimes other groups—from entire communities. As part of the deepening racism that swept through the United States after 1890, town after town outside the traditional South[2] became intentionally all-white.

This happened in two waves. First, an epidemic of attacks against Chinese Americans across the West prompted what I call the "Chinese Retreat," resulting in the concentration of that minority in Chinatowns in Seattle, San Francisco, Los Angeles, and a few other cities.[3] Then whites began forcing African Americans out of towns and rural areas across the North. This resulted in what I hope becomes generally recognized as the "Great Retreat"— the withdrawal of African Americans from towns and counties across the United States to black ghettoes in large northern cities.

Aching to Be All-White

How a problem is formulated influences how it gets thought about and what qualifies as a solution. After 1890, as we have seen, most whites no longer viewed slavery and racism as the problem—slavery was over, after all, and racial discrimination had been made illegal under the Fourteenth and Fifteenth Amendments. Now African Americans themselves were seen as the problem, by white northerners as well as southerners. Outside the traditional South, few whites now argued that their town *should* be interracial, as Republicans had done during Reconstruction. Whites now ached to be rid of their African Americans. The editor of the *Cairo Bulletin* summarized the feelings of white residents of Cairo, at the southern tip of Illinois, in 1920:

> "CAIRO DISAPPOINTED"
>
> Cairo's population on January 1, 1920, was 15,203, a gain of 655, or 4.5 per cent. This announcement was made by the Census bureau at Washington yesterday morning and transmitted to the *Bulletin* by Associated Press.
>
> The Population in 1910 was 14,548.
>
> Disappointment was expressed by some that the figure was not larger but those who knew how the population was made up were gratified at the showing. It is estimated that more than 2,000 Negroes have left Cairo since the last census, making the increase in the white population nearly 2,700 people.

Although "disappointed" that Cairo's overall population had gained only 4.5%, white residents were "gratified"[4] at its now whiter makeup.[5]

This line of thought was hardly unique to Cairo. During the first half of the twentieth century, towns competed by advertising how white they were; several Portfolio items show examples. In its *1907 Guide and Directory,* Rogers, Arkansas, bragged about what it had, including "seven churches, two public schools, one Academy, one sanitorium, ice plant and cold storage, etc.," and also what it did not have: "Rogers has no Negroes or saloons." Not to be outdone, nearby Siloam Springs claimed "Healing Waters, Beautiful Parks, Many Springs, Public Library," alongside "No Malaria, No Mosquitoes, and No Negroes." Whites in Cumberland County, Tennessee, forced out African Americans around 1900; in the 1920s, its main newspaper, the *Crossville Chronicle,* boasted, "No Mosquitoes, No Malaria, and No Niggers."

White residents of much of Oklahoma and the "non-southern" parts of Texas adopted this rhetoric. Land owners and developers who were trying to entice whites to central and western Texas in the 1910s exhorted them to "leave the niggers, chiggers, and gravediggers behind you!" Terry County, Texas, advertised itself in 1908 as a sundown county:

> Terry County is thirty miles square, situated eighty miles north from Stanton, on the T & P railroad, and about eighty southwest from Plainview, terminus of

the Santa Fe; was organized in 1904, and has about 2,000 population. ALL WHITE, about 400 homes . . .

Comanche County, Texas, drove out its African Americans in 1886. It was delighted also to have no Jews, almost no Mexicans, and few immigrants from southern and eastern Europe. After the 1940 U.S. Census, Representative Bill Chambers announced that according to a congressional report, "Comanche County, long famous for many unique advantages, has gained national distinction, for being the home of the purest Anglo-Saxon population of any county in the United States." Among its 19,245 residents, just 28 were born in countries other than the United States, including only 2 from Mexico, both listed as white.[6]

Many towns in the Midwest were likewise thrilled to be all-white. After bragging about high literacy and home ownership rates, the 1936 *Owosso and Shiawassee County Directory* in Owosso, Michigan, declared, "There is not a Negro living in the limits of Owosso's incorporated territory." Mentone, Indiana, bragged, "With a population of 1,100, Mentone has not a Catholic, foreigner, Negro, nor Jew living in the city." In its 1954 pamphlet titled "Royal Oak: Michigan's Most Promising Community," the Detroit suburb's Chamber of Commerce proudly proclaimed, "The population is virtually 100% white."[7]

The Far West was equally smitten with the idea. Fliers for Maywood Colony, a huge development entirely surrounding the town of Corning, California, trumpeted:

GOOD PEOPLE

In most communities in California you'll find Chinese, Japs, Dagoes, Mexicans, and Negroes mixing up and working in competition with the white folks. Not so at Maywood Colony. Employment is not given to this element.[8]

Thus except in the traditional South, driving African Americans out and keeping them out became the proper civic-minded thing to do, in the thinking of many whites of all social strata between about 1890 and 1940, lasting until at least 1968. Doing so seemed a perfectly reasonable solution once African Americans were defined as "the problem." Spurred by the ideological developments of the Nadir, towns with no black residents—including some with little prospect of attracting any—now passed ordinances or informally agreed that African Americans were not to be allowed after sundown. Where blacks did live, whites now forced them to flee from town after town, county after county, even entire regions—the Great Retreat. Threat of mob attack dangled over every black neighborhood in the nation (as it had earlier over most Chinese neighborhoods) as an ever-present menace. In short, an epidemic of sundown towns and counties swept America between 1890 and about 1940.

The Chinese Retreat

Before African Americans made their Great Retreat, the Chinese provided something of a dress rehearsal. Until about 1884, Chinese Americans lived in virtually every town in the West.[9] They were farmers and domestic servants, played a major role in the California fishing industry, and mined gold along streams in countryside newly wrested from the Indians. Hundreds of Chinese Americans mined coal in Wyoming in the 1870s. Their role in building the railroad and many other construction projects is well known. Republicans usually defended their right to immigrate to America and compete for employment.

Capitalists benefited from the competition, of course, but white workers did not, frequently resulting in sundown towns. Between 1885 and about 1920, dozens of communities in the West, including towns and counties as far inland as Wyoming and Colorado and cities as large as Seattle and Tacoma, drove out their entire Chinese American populations—some briefly, some for decades.

Rock Springs, Wyoming, built at a coal mine owned by the Union Pacific that was the biggest single source of coal for its locomotives, was the site of one of the earliest expulsions. The railroad had hired hundreds of Chinese American miners, most of whom lived in a separate neighborhood, "Chinatown." On September 2, 1885, led by the Knights of Labor, at least 150 white miners and railroad workers, most of them armed, gave the Chinese "one hour to pack their belongings and leave town," according to historian Craig Storti. Then they attacked. "The Chinamen were fleeing like a herd of hunted antelope, making no resistance. Volley upon volley was fired after the fugitives," Storti tells. It was chaotic: "Most carried nothing at all, not even their money." Many hid in their homes, but the rioters then burned Chinatown, incinerating those who were hiding there. Storti quotes an eyewitness:

> The stench of burning human flesh was sickening and almost unendurable, and was plainly discernible for more than a mile along the railroad both east and west. . . . Not a living Chinaman—man, woman, or child—was left in the town where 700 to 900 had lived the day before, and not a single house, shanty, or

structure of any kind that had ever been inhabited by a Chinaman was left unburned.

Those who fled were hardly better off, because the temperature dropped below freezing that night, so scores died from exposure. According to Bill Bryson, this persecution in Rock Springs led to the expression "He doesn't have a Chinaman's chance." Copycat riots and expulsions then swept the West, including almost every town in Wyoming; Cripple Creek and later Silverton, Colorado; Hells Canyon, Oregon; Grass Creek and Corinne, Utah; and communities in most other western states.[10]

The retreat of Chinese residents from Idaho was especially striking. In 1870, Chinese made up one-third of the population of Idaho. By 1910, almost none remained. In the 1880s, assaults and murder became common practice. In 1886, white Idahoans held an anti-Chinese convention in Boise, and a mass movement against the Chinese spread throughout the state, growing even worse after statehood in 1890. Historian Priscilla Wegars tells that in 1891, "all 22 Chinese in Clark Fork were run out of town," followed by Hoodoo the same year, Bonners Ferry in 1892, Coeur d'Alene in 1894, and Moscow in 1909. Chinese returned to some towns within a year or two but stayed out of Moscow until the mid-1920s and Coeur d'Alene until at least 1931.[11]

Around this time, Chinese in California also came under attack. Democrats supported white workers' attempts to exclude them. In May 1876, whites drove out Chinese from Antioch, California, one of the early expulsions, and in Rocklin the next year, they burned Chinatown to the ground. Expulsions and anti-Chinese ordinances peaked in the 1880s but continued for decades. In the 1890s whites violently expelled Chinese people from the fishing industry in most parts of the state. In all, between about 1884 and 1900, according to Jean Pfaelzer's careful research, more than 40 California towns drove all their Chinese residents out of town and kept them out. Around 1905 came Visalia's turn: whites "burned down the whole Chinatown," according to a man born there in 1900 who remembered that it happened when he was small. In June 1906, the city council of Santa Ana, California, passed a resolution that called for "the fire department to burn each and every one of the said buildings known as Chinatown"; on June 26 a crowd of more than a thousand watched it burn. Many of these towns enacted policies excluding Chinese Americans and remained "Chinese-free" for decades.[12]

One of the better-studied expulsions was from Eureka, in Humboldt County in northern California. On February 6, 1885, a city councilman was killed by a stray bullet fired by one of two quarreling Chinese men. White workers had already been clamoring, "The Chinese must go." That night, some 600 whites met to demand that all Chinese leave Humboldt County within 24 hours. Some white citizens defended the Chinese and tried to keep their own domestic servants but were forced to give them up. The next morning, some 480 Chinese and whatever belongings they could carry were aboard two steamships that then sailed for San Francisco. A week later, "a large crowd assembled at Centennial Hall to hear the report of the citizens' committee," according to Lynwood Carranco, who wrote a detailed account of the incident. They adopted several resolutions:

1) That all Chinamen be expelled from the city and that none be allowed to return.
2) That a committee be appointed to act for one year, whose duty shall be to warn all Chinamen who may attempt to come to this place to live, and to use all reasonable means to prevent their remaining. If the warning is disregarded, to call mass meetings of citizens to whom the case will be referred for proper action.
3 That a notice be issued to all property owners through the daily papers, requesting them not to lease or rent property to Chinese.[13]

Copycat expulsions followed from Arcata, Ferndale, and Crescent City (Portfolio 1 shows a broadside advocating "ridding Crescent City of Chinese"). By October 1906, some 23 Chinese workers had returned to work in a cannery in Humboldt County; they lasted less than a month before whites again drove them out. (Portfolio 2 shows this expulsion.) In 1937 the *Humboldt Times* published a souvenir edition on its 85th anniversary that bragged about its Chinese-free status:

Humboldt County has the unique distinction of being the only community in which there are no Oriental colonies. . . . [14] Although 52 years have passed since the Chinese were driven from the county, none have ever returned. On one or two occasions offshore vessels with Chinese crews have stopped at this port, but the Chinamen as a rule stayed aboard their vessels, choosing not to take a chance on being ordered out. Chinese everywhere have always looked upon this section of the state as "bad medicine" for the Chinamen.[15]

The attacks on Chinese in the West grew so bad that Mark Twain famously said, "A Chinaman had no rights that any man was bound to respect," deliberately echoing Roger Taney's words in *Dred Scott*. Whites even tried to drive out Chinese from large cities such as San Francisco and Seattle but failed, owing to the enormity of the task.[16]

The Chinese Retreat and the Great Retreat

From 1890 to the 1930s, whites across the North (and the nontraditional South) began to do to African Americans what westerners had done to Chinese Americans.[17] The Chinese retreat can be dated from the mid-1870s to about 1910, antedating the Great Retreat by fifteen to twenty years. There were other differences. Because Chinese Americans were not citizens, and because they had played no role in the Civil War, it was much harder for anti-racists to mobilize sentiment on their behalf. In 1879, only 900 California voters supported continued Chinese immigration, while 150,000 favored keeping them out. Also, municipal policies to keep out Chinese Americans mostly relaxed in the 1970s or even earlier, while sundown towns vis-à-vis African Americans lasted much longer.

However, there are at least seven close parallels between the two movements. First, Democrats led the attacks on both groups, in line with their position as the party of white supremacy. Second, there was some safety in numbers; ironically, some of the largest and most vicious race riots proved that. Although they tried, whites could not drive all Chinese Americans from Seattle, San Francisco, or Los Angeles. They succeeded in smaller places such as Rock Springs and Humboldt County. Similarly, blacks did find some refuge in majority-black neighborhoods in the inner city. Whites usually proved reluctant to venture far into alien territory to terrorize residents. Although whites attacked black neighborhoods in Chicago; East St. Louis, Illinois; Washington, D.C.; Tulsa; and other cities between 1917 and 1924, they were unable to destroy them for good.

Third, whites sometimes allowed one or two members of the despised race to stay, even as they forced out all others, especially if a rich white family protected them. Fourth, both groups often resisted being expelled or violated the bans. The 1906 return by Chinese Americans to Humboldt County offers a case in point; African Americans also returned repeatedly to towns that had driven them out. Fifth, after one town drove out or kept out Chinese Americans, whites in nearby towns often asked, "Why haven't *we* done that?" so an epidemic of expulsions resulted. Expulsions or prohibitions of African Americans likewise proved contagious, sweeping through whole regions. Sixth, once a community defined itself as a sundown town—vis-à-vis Chinese or

African Americans—typically it stayed that way for decades and celebrated its all-white status openly. Eureka did not repeal its anti-Chinese ordinance until 1959. Some sundown towns vis-à-vis African Americans *still* maintain their all-white status, although less openly than in the past.

Finally, and most important for our purposes, Chinatowns became the norm for Chinese American life only *after* the Chinese Retreat—about 1884 to 1910. Likewise, only after the Great Retreat did big-city ghettoes become the dwelling places of most northern blacks. African Americans were a *rural* people in the nineteenth century, and not just in the South, from which they moved, but also in the North, to which they came. In 1890 the proportion of black Illinoisans living in Chicago, for example (25%), was less than that for whites (29%). Nevertheless, by 1940 amnesia set in, and Americans forgot completely that in the nineteenth century, Chinese had lived in towns and hamlets throughout the West, while blacks had moved to little towns and rural areas across the North. Americans also repressed the memory of the expulsions and ordinances that created sundown towns. Now Americans typecast African Americans as residents of places such as Harlem and the South Side of Chicago, and Chinese Americans as Chinatown dwellers.[18]

In reality, white evictions and prohibitions provided the most important single reason for these retreats to large cities. In places where no such pressures existed, such as Mississippi, Chinese Americans continued to live throughout the Nadir period, sprinkled about in tiny rural towns such as Merigold and Louise; few lived in the metropolitan areas of Jackson or the Gulf Coast.[19]

The Great Retreat Was National

What happened next was national, not regional, and affected America's largest minority, far more than the 100,000 Chinese Americans then in the country. From town after town, county after county—even from whole regions—African Americans were driven by white opposition, winding up in huge northern ghettoes.

Sometimes this was accomplished by violence, sometimes by subtler means; the next chapter tells how sundown towns were created. Here it is important to understand that we are not talking about a handful of sundown towns sprinkled across America. The Great Retreat left in its wake a new geography of race in the United States. From Myakka City, Florida, to Kennewick, Washington, the nation is dotted with thousands of all-white towns that are (or were until recently) all white on purpose. Sundown towns can be found in almost every state.[20] This chapter takes us on a whirlwind journey around the United States, exploring sundown towns and counties in every region. Independent sundown towns are fairly common in the East, frighteningly so in the Midwest, nontraditional South, and Far West, but rare in the traditional South. Sundown suburbs are common everywhere, although they are now disappearing in the South and Far West. Indeed, because sundown towns proved to be so numerous, this chapter proved the hardest to write. If it described or even merely listed sundown towns by state, the chapter would become impossibly long, but if it only generalized about the extent of the problem, it would be unconvincing. I tried to find a middle path, a mix of examples and generalities, and set up a web site, uvm.edu/~jloewen/sundown, giving many more examples.

County Populations Show the Great Retreat

One way to show the Great Retreat is by examining the population of African Americans by county. Between 1890 and 1930 or 1940, the absolute number of African Americans in many northern counties and towns plummeted.[21] Table 1, "Counties with No or Few African Americans' in 1890 and 1930," shows this phenomenon in several ways. The "total" row at the bottom of the table shows that, as a result of the relatively welcoming atmosphere of the 1860s–80s, only 119 counties in the United States (excluding the traditional South) had no African American residents in 1890. *But by 1930, the number of counties with not a single African American had nearly doubled, to 235.* Counties with just a handful of African Americans (fewer than 10) also increased, from 452 in 1890 to 694 by 1930.[22] Many entire counties that had African Americans in 1890 had none by 1930. Other counties with sizable black populations in 1890 had only a handful of African Americans by 1930.

These findings fly in the face of normal population diffusion, which would predict continued dispersal over time. Thus the number of counties with no members of a group would normally decrease, even if no new members of the group entered the overall system, just from the ordinary haphazard moves of individuals and families from place to place. That the opposite happened is quite surprising and indicates the withdrawal of African Americans from many counties across the Northern states. Table 1 excludes the traditional South;[23] we shall see why shortly.

Table 1. Counties with No or Few (< 10) African Americans, 1890 and 1930

STATE	1890 0 BLACKS	1890 <10 BLACKS	1930 0 BLACKS	1930 <10 BLACKS
Arizona	0	1	1	1
Arkansas	0	1	3	8
California	0	4	0	8
Colorado	5	19	8	28
Connecticut	0	0	0	0
Delaware	0	0	0	0
Idaho	1	9	14	33
Illinois	0	6	6	17
Indiana	1	14	6	20
Iowa	13	28	12	38
Kansas	6	20	6	23
Kentucky	0	0	0	4
Maine	0	2	0	5
Maryland	0	0	0	0
Massachusetts	0	0	0	0
Michigan	4	23	7	26
Minnesota	22	57	16	61
Missouri	0	8	12	28
Montana	0	2	11	41
Nebraska	9	41	28	64
Nevada	1	6	1	8
New Hampshire	0	0	0	2
New Jersey	0	0	0	0
New Mexico	0	9	3	11
New York	0	0	0	1
North Dakota	13	26	20	42
Ohio	0	1	1	2
Oklahoma	2	10	4	11
Oregon	1	16	4	24
Pennsylvania	0	3	1	4
Rhode Island	0	0	0	0
South Dakota	19	37	23	52
Texas	3	20	8	29
Utah	5	16	15	22
Vermont	0	3	1	4
Washington	5	16	6	20
West Virginia	1	3	1	4
Wisconsin	8	27	16	42
Wyoming	0	5	1	11
Total	119	456	235	694

Boldface indicates states with more counties with 0 or few blacks in 1930 than in 1890.

The striking uniformity in Table 1 also reveals the startling extent of the Great Retreat. Beginning at the top, we note that every Arizona county had at least one African American in 1910, the first year for which data exist. But by 1930, one Arizona county has no African Americans at all. One county is not worth reporting, but the trend grows more pronounced in Arkansas, which also had no county without African Americans in 1890 but had three by 1930, as well as five more with just a handful. The pattern then holds with remarkable consistency in California, Colorado, and all the rest. Of the 39 states in the table, *not one showed greater dispersion of African Americans in 1930 than in 1890. In 31 of 39 states, African Americans lived in a narrower range of counties in 1930 than they did in 1890.* Minnesota showed a mixed result,[24] and seven states—Connecticut, Delaware, Maryland, Massachusetts, New Jersey, New York, and Rhode Island—had virtually no counties in either year with fewer than ten blacks, so they could show no trend in Table 1. However, the Appendix provides a closer look at those eight states and reveals that there, too, African Americans concentrated in just a few counties in 1930, to a far greater extent than did whites.[25] *Thus those states also fit the pattern; hence every state in Table 1 shows some confirmation of the Great Retreat.*

Some of the statewide retreats indicated in Table 1 are dramatic. For example, African Americans lived in every Indiana county but one in 1890. By 1930, six counties had none and another fourteen had fewer than ten African American residents, even though many more African Americans now lived in the state. I have confirmed eighteen Indiana counties as sundown throughout or in substantial part. Moreover, even when Table 1 does not show a dramatic decline, looking at the actual number of African Americans in each county does. For example, in 1890, every county in the state of Maine had at least eighteen African Americans, except one with just two and another with nine. By 1930, Maine looked very different. Now five counties had eight or fewer African Americans. Several showed striking drops in their black populations: Lincoln County from 26 to 5, for example, and Piscataquis from 19 to just 1. Hancock County dropped from 56 in 1890 to just 3, yet Hancock had more than 30,000 people in 1930. Geography does not seem to account for these declines; the counties with fewer than eight African Americans were sprinkled about, not concentrated in Maine's isolated rural north.

The Great Retreat and the Great Migration

These decreases to no or only a few African Americans by 1930 came in the teeth of huge increases in the black population nationally and in many northern states. Nationally, the number of African Americans went up by nearly 60%, from 7,388,000 in 1890 to 11,759,000 in 1930. Moreover, beginning about 1915, African Americans from Dixie started moving north in large numbers, a movement now known as the "Great Migration," in response to the impact of World War I, which simultaneously increased the demand for American products abroad and interfered with European migration to north-ern cities.[26] More than 1,000,000 African Americans moved north between 1915 and 1930. Thus the absolute declines in black population by 1930 in many northern counties are all the more staggering. Without a retreat to the cities, these increases in overall black populations would have caused the number of counties with zero or few blacks to plummet.

Coming in the middle of the deepening racism of the Nadir, this Great Migration prompted even more white northerners to view African Americans as a threat. A 1916 editorial from Beloit, Wisconsin, exemplifies the "Negro as problem" rhetoric:

> The Negro problem has moved north. Rather, the Negro problem has spread from south to north. . . . Within a few years, experts predict the Negro popula-tion of the North will be tripled. It's your problem, or it will be when the Negro moves next door. . . . With the black tide setting north, the southern Negro, formerly a docile tool, is demanding better pay, better food, and better treat-ment. . . . It's a national problem now, instead of a sectional problem. And it has got to be solved.[27]

Historians and sociologists took note of the growing urban concentration of African Americans between 1890 and 1930, continuing to about 1960. One of the foremost writers on race relations of the era, T. J. Woofter Jr., put it this way: "It is remarkable that Negro city population should have increased by a million and a half between 1900 and 1920; but it is astounding that a mil-lion of this increase should have been concentrated in the metropolitan cen-ters of the East and the Middle West." More than half of this increase was absorbed by just 24 cities, each having black populations of more than 25,000, he observed. "This emphasizes the astonishing degree of concentra-tion that has taken place."[28]

But neither Woofter nor other commentators noted the *decreases* in black populations—often to zero or to a single household—in smaller cities and towns across the North. The Great Migration seems to have masked the Great Retreat. Scores of books discuss the Great Migration; none tells of the Great Retreat (by this or any other name). The increased black population in, say,

Chicago got ascribed to migration from Mississippi, which was largely true; hence the internal migration of African Americans from small towns in Illinois to Chicago went unnoticed. Not grasping the extent of anti-black sentiment in smaller northern towns during the Nadir, social scientists somehow found it "natural" for people from tiny Glen Allan, Mississippi, to wind up in Chicago; for those from Brownsville, Tennessee, to move to Decatur, Illinois; and for inhabitants of Ninety Six, South Carolina, to move to Washington, D.C. This is not how other migrations to the North worked. People from small villages in Italy often wound up in places such as Barre, Vermont, or West Frankfort, Illinois, as well as St. Louis. Norwegians went to Mount Horeb, Wisconsin, not just Minneapolis. But this was not true of African Americans—not after the 1890s, anyway.

Indeed, historians and social scientists have used the Great Migration to "explain" the increased racism in the North. That is, they used documents such as the Beloit editorial to explain the increased segregation African Americans experienced: the masses of newcomers strained the system, threatened whites' jobs, upset existing equilibriums, and the like. But the Great Migration did not cause the Great Retreat. Whites were already driving African Americans from small towns across the Midwest *before* those towns experienced any substantial migration from the South. They continued to drive out blacks from towns that never saw any sizable influx after 1915. The Great Retreat started in 1890, a product of the increasing white racism of the Nadir. It cannot be understood as a reaction to a migration that started in 1915.

Now let us tour the country, seeing the profusion of sundown towns almost everywhere, beginning in the Midwest. In the process, we shall visit towns that excluded not only African Americans, but also Chinese, Jewish, Native, and Mexican Americans—and in a few cases Catholics, labor union members, homosexuals, and some others. We shall see that prime real estate—elite suburbs, beach resorts, mountain vacation spots, and islands—has typically been off-limits. And we shall encounter whole subregions where African Americans are generally not allowed, even in unincorporated rural areas.

The Great Retreat in the Heartland

I did more research in Illinois than in any other single state. Table 1 shows that African Americans lived in every Illinois county in 1890. By 1930, six counties had none, while another eleven had fewer than ten African American residents. Without a doubt, exclusion underlies these numbers. In Illinois and elsewhere, entire counties developed and enforced the policy of keeping out

African Americans. Many of the towns confirmed as sundown towns in my research are county seats, and when they went sundown, often—not always— the rest of the county followed suit. I have confirmed that ten of these seventeen counties had gone sundown by 1930 and suspect all seventeen[29] did.

Various written and oral sources tell of Illinois counties that kept out African Americans as a matter of county policy. Malcolm Ross of the Fair Employment Practices Commission wrote about Calhoun County, for example, "Calhoun County is recorded in the 1940 census as '8,207 whites; no Negroes; no other races.' This is not by accident. Calhoun people see to it that no Negroes settle there." According to an 83-year-old lifelong resident of Mason County, north of Springfield, the sheriff "would meet [blacks] at the county line and tell them not to come in."[30] Mason County has remained all white for many decades, despite its location between Springfield and Peoria, both with large African American populations, and on the Illinois River, an important trade route.[31]

Table 1 is a useful way to summarize the entire northern United States, but county data can only hint at the extent of the problem, because county is such a broad unit of analysis. Illinois may have had seventeen sundown counties in 1930, but it had far more sundown towns than that. Several entire counties in Illinois allowed no African Americans except in one or two isolated locations, for example, but that one place sufficed to remove such a county from Table 1. Town is a more useful jurisdiction to examine. Most sundown towns in Illinois lie in counties that never appear in Table 1. In 1970, when sundown towns were probably at their maximum, Illinois had 621 towns larger than 1,000 people, ranging from Wyanet, with 1,005, to Chicago.[32] Of these, 424 or almost 70% were "all-white" (as defined in Chapter 1) in census after census. In addition, my universe of towns must include 50 hamlets smaller than 1,000 that came to my attention because of evidence confirming them as sundown towns. Therefore my list of Illinois towns totaled 671, ranging from tiny hamlets to Chicago. Of these 671 towns, 474 or 71% were all-white,[33] while 197 had African Americans.

Of course, the mere fact that they were all-white does not confirm the 474 as sundown towns. That requires information as to their racial policies in the past. I was able to get such material on 146 of the 424 all-white towns larger than 1,000. Of these 146, I have confirmed 145 as sundown towns or suburbs, or 99.5%.[34] In addition, the 50 hamlets smaller than 1,000 in population were confirmed as sundown towns. Confirmed Illinois sundown towns range in size from communities of just a few hundred people to Cicero, which in 1970[35] had 67,058 residents, and Pekin, which in 1970 had 31,375 and another 3,500 in its suburbs.

If 145 of the 146 suspected sundown towns larger than 1,000 on which we have information indeed turned out to be confirmed, what can we predict about the remaining 278 towns, on which we have no historical information beyond census data? Our best estimate would be that 99.5%— the same proportion as among the towns we have checked out—or about 277 of them would be sundown towns. There is no good reason to suppose the next towns will be different from those we know.[36] When we add to that estimate of 277 the 145 towns that I have confirmed, plus the 50 hamlets, *our best single estimate is that 472 of the 474 all-white towns and hamlets were all-white on purpose.*

Of course, we would not be surprised if "only" 465 (98%) of the 474 towns turned out to be sundown, or if 473 were sundown. Applying the principles of inferential statistics, we can calculate a range within which we can be confident the true number of sundown towns will fall. Statisticians call this the "confidence limits" for our best estimate of 472 or 99.5%.[37] They find these limits by computing the statistical formula known as the standard error of the difference of two percentages. Here this standard error equals .0205 or 2.05%.[38] The more rigorous confidence band used by statisticians is the 99% limit, the range that is large enough that we can be 99% sure that it includes the true proportion of sundown towns among the unknown towns. Here that range is 5.3%.[39] Accordingly, our estimate for the correct proportion of sundown towns among the unexamined towns would be .995 ± .053 or 94.2% to 104.8%. Of course, numbers above 100% are impossible; we can be 99% confident that the number of sundown towns among the unknown towns is roughly 94% to 100%, or 261 to 278 of the 278 towns.[40] Adding the 195 known sundown towns yields an overall estimate that the number of sundown towns among all 474 overwhelmingly white towns in Illinois lies between 456 (96%) and 473 (99.8%). We can say with a 99% level of confidence that between 96% and 99.8% of all the all-white towns in Illinois were sundown towns.[41] Our best single estimate remains 472, or 99.5%.

Even this total, 472, is not the full number of sundown towns in Illinois. I included communities smaller than 1,000 inhabitants only when informants or written sources brought them to my attention. These 50 confirmed sundown hamlets persuaded me to be suspicious of even very small all-white communities; many other hamlets no doubt kept out blacks.[42] Also, various sundown towns larger than 1,000 in population missed getting on my radar in the first place,[43] owing to nonhousehold African Americans such as prisoners.

These sundown towns are spread out throughout the state. Southern Illinois had many more even than Map 1 shows. Central Illinois has just as many: oral history confirmed some three dozen communities as sundown towns just within a 60-mile radius of Decatur, and written documentation confirmed another dozen. Northern Illinois has even more, owing to the sundown suburbs ringing Chicago. As a correspondent suggested about Ohio, instead of studying sundown towns, perhaps I should have researched the exceptions—towns that never excluded blacks—since that would be a more manageable number.

Similar maps could be drawn, showing most towns in boldface, in most other states in the Midwest, the Ozarks, the Cumberlands, the suburbs of any city from Boston to Los Angeles, and many other areas of the United States. But before we leave Illinois, this statistic of 472 probable sundown towns might come alive if I supply examples. I have chosen three, one from each section of the state.

LaSalle and Peru in northern Illinois are separate towns, each with its own library, city hall, etc., but they share a high school and a common boundary, and most people consider them really one entity. I don't know when they first became sundown towns. Not one African American lived in the towns on the eve of the Civil War, when their combined population was 8,279. Even back then, the absence of blacks was surprising, since both towns lie on the Illinois River, a major artery, and on the Illinois-Michigan Canal, connecting Lake Michigan to the river at Peru, which opened up a water route from New Orleans to the Great Lakes. By 1860, when railroads became dominant, LaSalle-Peru found itself equally favored, being on a main line of the Illinois Central as well as the Rock Island Line, a major east-west railroad from Chicago. These trade routes surely would have brought African Americans to LaSalle-Peru had they been allowed. In 1864, seven African Americans from nearby Mendota signed up for the army and traveled with their recruiting officer to LaSalle to go up the canal to Joliet to be mustered in. In LaSalle a gang of "Copperheads" attacked them and drove them out of the city.[44] Census takers in 1870 found only one African American in Peru, none in LaSalle. Yet the war had caused many African Americans to wind up in Cairo, whence they diffused through the Midwest, and the Illinois Central directly connects Mississippi, Cairo, and LaSalle-Peru. In 1880, LaSalle was the only city in Illinois (defined as larger than 4,000 in that year) with no African Americans, and Peru was one of only two cities that had just one. An 1889 article in the

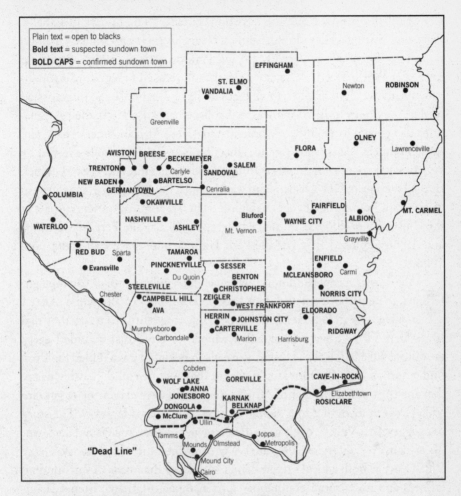

Map 1. Centers of Manufacturing in Southern Illinois

In 1952 Charles Colby mapped 80 communities in southern Illinois—including every larger city, many towns, and some hamlets—all chosen because they had factories. Identifying their racial policies shows how widespread sundown towns were, at least in this subregion. Of his 80 towns, 55 or 69% are suspected sundown towns, "all-white" for decades. Among these 55, I confirmed the racial policies of 52, and of those 52, 51 (all but Newton) were sundown towns.

The dotted line at the bottom is the "dead line," north of which African Americans were not allowed to live (except in the unbolded towns). South of this line, cotton was the major crop; white landowners employed black labor, following the southern tradition of hierarchical race relations rather than northern sundown policies. All 8 towns below this line allowed African Americans to live in them. Among the 72 towns above the line, only 18—a quarter—did so to my knowledge.

Chicago Tribune noted that this was no accident: "The miners of LaSalle, Peru, and Spring Valley do not allow a Negro in their city limits." Around this time, the towns apparently posted sundown signs, which stayed up until after World War II. The cities clearly still refused to let African Americans spend the night in 1952, for in that year its high school band director had to skirt the policy to host an integrated college band. By 1970, their populations had grown to 22,508, of whom just five were African American. Again, these numbers are shockingly low, since the cities were now also served by U.S. 6, a major east-west highway from Atlantic to Pacific, and U.S. 51, which runs all the way to New Orleans and was the most important single highway in Mississippi before the advent of the interstate system. An undergraduate at the University of Illinois-Chicago who grew up in LaSalle-Peru in the 1980s and 1990s reported that LaSalle-Peru High School stayed all-white until 1998.[45]

Villa Grove, a central Illinois town seventeen miles south of Champaign-Urbana, is newer and smaller than LaSalle-Peru, but equally white. After I spoke in Decatur in October 2001, two people came forward to say they had heard that Villa Grove had or has a whistle or siren that sounded every evening at 6 PM to tell all African Americans to be out of town. I filed the story under "urban legends," thinking it absurd that anyone could possibly worry that any substantial number of African Americans were clamoring to get *into* Villa Grove, a town of 2,553 people located on no major highway. The story did suggest that Villa Grove is a sundown town, however, so I visited the town. To my surprise, interview after interview confirmed the whistle story. Today Villa Grove is both a local service center supplying the needs of surrounding farmers and a bedroom community for Champaign-Urbana. Some Champaign-Urbana residents moved to Villa Grove and now commute to work to minimize their contact with African Americans in Champaign-Urbana. One African American woman at the University of Illinois told of conversations with a white colleague at her former job. He was a native of Villa Grove, as was his wife, from whom he had separated. As he recounted it, his wife insisted that he wash his hands at her home before picking up their daughters for weekend visitation, because she knew an African American was employed at his workplace and they might have touched common objects.[46]

In July 1899, striking white miners drove a group of African American strikebreakers down the railroad tracks out of Carterville, a town of 3,600 in southern Illinois. In the process, they shot five of them dead. Eventually the whites were all acquitted, the strikers won, and all African Americans were forced to leave. Carterville had already pushed the sundown town concept to a new level before 1899, not permitting African Americans to set foot inside the city limits, even during the day. This policy remained in force for decades. Even Dr. Andrew Springs, the black physician serving Dewmaine, a small black community about a mile north of Carterville, had to wait at the edge of town in the 1930s for drugs he had ordered from Carterville's pharmacy to be delivered to him. In the late 1970s, the first black family moved in. According to Carl Planinc, who has lived in Carterville for several decades, "ironically, their first night, there was a fire, and their house burned down."[47]

Stories such as these exist for each town that I list as confirmed, and I believe similar information, differing only in detail, remains to be harvested from almost every one of Illinois's 474 all-white towns. What about other states? Roberta Senechal, one of the handful of authors who have mentioned sundown towns, noted that "such banning of blacks by custom and unwritten law from rural and small-town communities was not a phenomenon limited to Illinois." She is right, of course, so I widened my circle, turning first to Indiana, next door.[48]

Indiana showed a similar pattern. Of course, of all states, Indiana is most like Illinois and borders it for 300 miles. In 1964, in an affectionate memoir, *My Indiana,* Irving Leibowitz wrote, "Intolerance was everywhere. 'NIGGER, DON'T LET THE SUN SET ON YOU HERE,' was a sign posted in most every small town in Indiana." As in Illinois, whole Indiana counties kept out African Americans entirely or restricted them to one or two small hamlets.[49] Map 2 shows eighteen confirmed sundown counties and fifteen suspects in 1970. In addition, many confirmed sundown towns lie sprinkled across Indiana's unshaded counties.[50]

Some Indiana sundown towns were famous for their policy. Elwood's moment of notoriety as a sundown town came in 1940 when native son Wendell Willkie was nominated for president there. Its population was then 11,000; as many as 150,000 people crowded in for the rally. Frances Peacock wrote a memoir about two black Republicans who never made it, George Sawyer and his father:

> In 1940 George and his father, an active Republican, were on their way to Elwood, Indiana, to attend a rally for Wendell Willkie, the Republican presidential candidate. When they arrived at Elwood that morning before the convention, they saw two road signs posted at the city limits: "Niggers, read this and run. If you can't read, run anyhow," and "Nigger, don't let the sun set on you in Elwood."

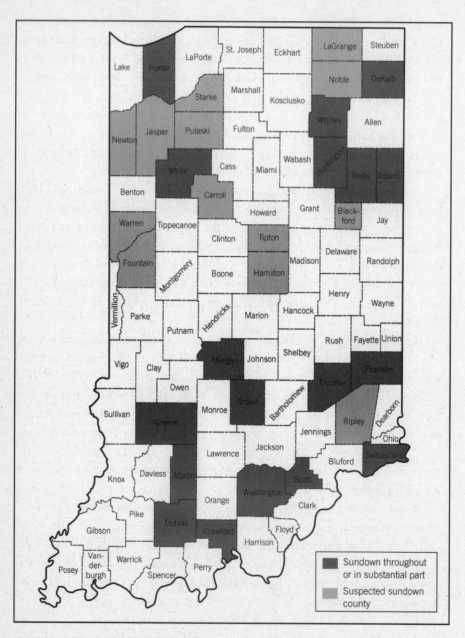

Map 2. Sundown Counties in Indiana

Indiana had only 1 black-free county in 1890, but 6 by 1930, as well as 27 others with a handful of African Americans. All 33 were probably sundown counties; I have confirmed 18.

George's father turned the car around and drove back to Anderson. And from then on, he was a Democrat.[51]

I identified a total of 231 Indiana towns as all-white.[52] I was able to get information as to the racial policies of 95, and of those, I confirmed all 95 as sundown towns.[53] In Indiana, I have yet to uncover *any* overwhelmingly white town that on-site research failed to confirm as a sundown town. Ninety-five out of 95 is an astounding proportion; statistical analysis shows that it is quite likely that 90 to 100% of all 231 were sundown towns. They ranged from tiny hamlets to cities in the 10,000–50,000 population range, including Huntington (former vice president Dan Quayle's hometown) and Valparaiso (home of Valparaiso University).

Portfolio 25 shows the last page from the 1970 census for Indiana towns with 1,000 to 2,499 residents.[54] Note the striking number of dashes in the "Negro" column—towns that had not a single African American. Surely Leibowitz was right. Indeed, almost four decades after Leibowitz wrote, my research uncovered oral or written history, usually from more than one source, of actual sundown signs posted in at least 21 Indiana communities.[55] Most had come down by the end of World War II, but according to Mike Haas, signs in the little town of Sunman said "NIGGER! BETTER NOT BE SEEN HERE AFTER SUNDOWN!" until well into the 1980s. The most recent sign was spotted in White County in 1998.[56]

Intentionally all-white communities dot the rest of the Midwest. In Ohio, independent sundown towns are found from Niles in the north to Syracuse on the Ohio River, and sundown suburbs proliferate around Cincinnati and Cleveland. Missouri has an extraordinary number of sundown towns, at least 200. Many are in the Ozarks and will be treated later in this chapter, but the more midwestern parts of Missouri have dozens of sundown towns and counties as well. In sum, by 1930 probably a majority of all towns in the heartland kept out African Americans. No wonder blacks moved to Chicago and St. Louis.

Sundown Towns in the Far North

Clearly sundown towns were a phenomenon throughout the lower Midwest. But what about states farther north? Ohio, Indiana, and Illinois border former slave states, after all, and Missouri was a slave state, so they were near black populations. Initially I did not expect to find sundown towns in far northern states such as Maine, Michigan, Wisconsin, Idaho, or Oregon. I labored

under the misapprehension that all-white towns so far north were unlikely to
be purposeful. I thought that because these states were so distant from African
American population centers, it may be unreasonable to expect their towns to
have black residents in the first place. Also I imagined that whites so far north,
faced with no possible "threat" from any large number of African Americans,
would be unlikely to adopt exclusionary policies. I was wrong on both counts.

Take Wisconsin, for example, not usually considered a place where
African Americans concentrated, except perhaps Milwaukee. In 1890, the
state was indeed only 0.15% black. Nevertheless, before 1890, black people
hardly limited themselves to Milwaukee. Table 1 shows that only 8 of Wisconsin's 68 counties held no African Americans in 1890; another 27 counties had
fewer than 10. Twenty-six counties had at least twenty African Americans, and
these were sprinkled about the state. Four counties around Lake Winnebago—
Calumet, Fond du Lac, Outagamie, and Winnebago—boasted 389 African
Americans among them, almost as many as Milwaukee. In all, 1,986 African
Americans lived outside of Milwaukee, along with 458 black Milwaukeeans.

By 1930, the number of African Americans living in Milwaukee had
swelled almost tenfold to 4,188, while outside Milwaukee lived fewer blacks—
just 1,623—than in 1890. In 1890, less than 20% of Wisconsin's African
Americans lived in Milwaukee; by 1930, 72% did. The most dramatic declines came in the counties around Lake Winnebago, by 1930 home to just 86
African Americans, most of them in Winnebago County. Fond du Lac's 178
African Americans in 1880 dwindled to just 22 in 1930 and 5 by 1940.
Statewide, 16 counties had no African Americans at all by 1930, and another
42 had fewer than ten.

Among its 144 cities of more than 2,500 population in 1970, Wisconsin
had 126 all-white communities (as defined in Chapter 1). No prior published
histories treat the phenomenon of sundown towns in Wisconsin, so far as I
know, and I could not spend nearly as much time doing oral history in Wisconsin as in Illinois and Indiana. Nevertheless, I confirmed nine as sundown
towns; for ten others, including several towns near Lake Winnebago, I have
some evidence.[57] I am sure that many additional Wisconsin towns, including
several Milwaukee suburbs, also excluded African Americans, but have not
done on-site research to prove it.

Some Wisconsin sundown towns were tiny hamlets; even some unincorporated rural locales kept out African Americans by refusing to sell them land
or hire them as farm labor. Some were startingly large cities, such as Appleton,
population 60,000, and Sheboygan, 45,000.[58] Sheboygan, for example, acted
as if it had passed a sundown ordinance: it had a police officer meet trains at

the railroad station to warn African Americans not to stay there, according to a resident there in the early 1960s. At least one town, Manitowoc, posted signs. Grey Gundaker, now a professor at the College of William and Mary, saw them when he lived there from 1962 to 1964: "The signs were worded approximately 'NIGGER: Don't let the sun go down on you in our town!' "he recalls. "I think the words were in italics and painted across a picture of a green hill with the sun setting halfway behind it."[59]

Beaver Dam, 60 miles northwest of Milwaukee, grew steadily from 4,222 people in 1890 to 10,356 in 1940 and 14,265 in 1970. Despite this growth, its black population fell from eight in 1890 to just one a decade later, then stayed at one or two until after 1970.[60] A 1969 report at Wayland Academy, a prep school located in Beaver Dam, evaluated "the feasibility of admitting Negroes to Wayland"; its authors interviewed townspeople "to determine problems which might face a Negro as he lives in this presently nonintegrated community." Several older inhabitants of Beaver Dam "all said the same thing in the same words" to Moira Meltzer-Cohen, Beaver Dam resident and resourceful researcher: " 'A couple of black families tried to move in during the '60s and '70s and they were run right out.' "[61]

Wisconsin exemplifies findings from other far north states. Oregon had just one county with no African Americans at all in 1890, although it had sixteen more with fewer than ten. By 1930, however, Oregon had four counties with no African Americans and twenty more with fewer than ten. Exclusion was responsible. Correspondents have sent me evidence confirming that a string of towns along what is now Interstate 5 in western Oregon, for instance, including Eugene, Umpqua, Grants Pass, Eagle Point, Medford, and others, kept out African Americans until the recent past. Other examples across the far north from west to east include Kennewick and Richland in Washington; Ashton and Wallace in Idaho, and probably all of Lemhi County; Austin, Minnesota; many towns in Michigan; and Tonawanda and North Tonawanda in New York, almost on the Canadian border. Wallace, for example, expelled its Chinese in the nineteenth century; in the twentieth it put up a sign at the edge of town that said "Nigger, Read This Sign and Run"; and in the 2000 census it still had no African Americans and just one Asian American. So even in the Idaho panhandle up by Canada, towns felt the need to keep out people of color.[62]

The Great Retreat Did Not Strike the "Traditional South"

Very different race relations evolved in what I call the "traditional South"— Virginia, North Carolina, South Carolina, Georgia, Florida, Alabama, Tennessee, Mississippi, and Louisiana, all states historically dominated by slavery.[63] There, in contrast to the North, slavery grew more entrenched after the American Revolution. Some whites grew wealthy from the unpaid labor, and most others yearned to emulate them. After slavery ended, the tradition continued in the form of sharecropping, which kept many blacks in peonage, unable to pay the perpetual debt by which white landowners bound them to the land. In towns, blacks continued to do the domestic chores, janitoring, and backbreaking work that whites avoided—now in exchange for inadequate wages. To hire blacks, whom they could pay less than whites, was in the interest of plantation owners, railroads, and other employers.

County populations in the traditional South do not show the Great Retreat. Indeed, during the Nadir, when sundown towns were most in vogue, whites from the traditional South expressed astonishment at the practice. Why expel your maid, your agricultural workforce, your school janitor, your railroad track layers? Writing about Washington County, Indiana, Emma Lou Thornbrough noted that African Americans "were not allowed to come in even as servants, a fact which occasioned surprise among visitors from the South." Traditional white southerners saw African Americans as workers to be exploited and sometimes as problems to be controlled but not expelled.[64]

Therefore the traditional South has almost no independent sundown towns, and never did. This does not make whites in the traditional South less racist than in other parts of the South or other regions of the country. Racist they were—indeed, racism arose in Western cultures primarily as a rationale for racial slavery—but the tradition entailed controlling and exploiting blacks, not getting rid of them. Indeed, the original sundown rule was a curfew at dusk during slavery times; to be out after dark, slaves had to have written passes from their owners. After slavery ended in the traditional South, whites often lynched African Americans to keep them down; elsewhere in the United States, whites sometimes lynched them, we will see, to drive them out.

Thus Mississippi, for example, has just two all-white towns with a population over 1,000, Belmont and Burnsville, and they lie barely in the state, in the northeast corner near the Alabama line, in Appalachia.[65] It also had three suburbs that excluded African Americans between 1945 and 1975. Alabama has two sundown counties and a handful of sundown towns, but all except one are in far north Alabama—in Appalachia, not in the traditional South— and the exception is a sundown suburb of Mobile.[66] Louisiana has a few, but they are tiny. The cotton culture part of Arkansas boasts not a single sundown town. California has more sundown towns than all parts of the traditional South put together. Illinois has many times more.

The Great Retreat from the Rest of the South

More like the Midwest and West is the "nontraditional South"—Appalachia, the Cumberlands, the Ozarks, much of Florida, and north and west Texas. There, huge swaths of counties, as well as many individual towns, drove out their African Americans beginning in about 1890.[67] Follansbee, West Virginia, for example, kept out African Americans "for years" before the early 1920s. Then some mills brought in African Americans as employees. In October 1923, the Ku Klux Klan burned two fiery crosses and painted a threat on the fence facing "the colored section," warning all blacks to leave immediately, according to the *Pittsburgh Courier*. They fled, and the sundown policy apparently remained in force, for in 2000, Follansbee had 3,115 people, but not a single African American household.[68]

Table 1 shows that much of the nontraditional South did expel its African Americans during the Nadir. Arkansas shows the difference dramatically. In 1890, it had no county without African Americans and only one with fewer than ten; by 1930, three counties had none and another eight had fewer than ten, all in the Arkansas Ozarks. I suspect all eleven were sundown counties and have confirmed six. If we draw a line from the southwest corner of Arkansas northeast to the Missouri Bootheel, the resulting triangle bordering Oklahoma and Missouri includes all 11 counties and all 74 suspected sundown towns in Arkansas. The southeastern part of the state, in contrast, where cotton culture dominated and secession sentiment was strongest, includes not a single sundown town or county.

Similarly, most sundown towns and counties in Texas are in north Texas or southwest of Fort Worth, rather than in the traditionally southern areas of East Texas. Maryland, Kentucky, and Missouri also show this pattern: their sundown towns are in the hills and mountains or are suburbs. Maryland's one sundown county, Garrett, is its farthest west, in Appalachia. Garrett County doesn't show in Table 1 but had become overwhelmingly white by 1940. At least two far west counties in Virginia and two in North Carolina, along with two counties and several towns in east Tennessee, also went sundown after 1890. So did six counties in north Georgia—including Forsyth—and most of Winston County in northern Alabama. Indeed, the Great Retreat was particularly pronounced from the nontraditional South. Map 3 shows some of the areas in the nontraditional South where many counties and towns went sundown, almost all after about 1890.

In the first two decades of the twentieth century, whites expelled African Americans from almost the entire Cumberland Plateau, a huge area extending from the Ohio River near Huntington, West Virginia, southwest through Corbin, Kentucky, crossing into Tennessee, where it marks the division between east and middle Tennessee, and finally ending in northern Alabama. In most parts of the plateau throughout most of the twentieth century, when night came to the Cumberlands, African Americans had better be absent.[69] The twenty Cumberland counties in eastern Kentucky had 3,482 African Americans in 1890, or 2% of the region's 175,631 people. By 1930, although their overall population had increased by more than 50%, these counties had only 1,387 black residents. The decline continued: by 1960 the African American population of these counties had declined to just 531, or 0.2%, one-tenth the 1890 proportion.

Throughout the plateau, this decline was forced. Picking a few examples from north to south, Rockcastle County, Kentucky, had a sundown sign up as late as the mid-1990s, according to George Brosi, editor of *Appalachian Heritage.* In the 1990 census, Rockcastle had no African Americans among its 14,743 people. Esther Sanderson, historian of Scott County, Tennessee, made clear her county's policy:

> There was a big sign on the road at the Kentucky state line and at the entrance at Morgan County [the next county south]: "Nigger, don't let the sun set on your head." The Negroes rarely ever passed through; if they did, they made haste to get through.

Farther south, the sundown policy of Grundy County, Tennessee, garnered national attention in the 1950s when Myles Horton defied it and located his Highlander Folk School, famed for training civil rights leaders, there.[70] Highlander's interracial policy was unpalatable to the county, so in 1959 they got the Tennessee legislature to investigate the school. Eventually Grundy County took Highlander to court and forced the institution to leave, charging Horton with beer sales on its property. Did race have anything to do with it? Paul Cook, Grundy County resident and a member of the jury that found Highlander guilty, assures us it did not:

> That integration business, that didn't have anything to do with it. Lots of folks around here resent the colored, and we still don't have any in this county—but they'd have been in trouble without the niggers.

The Cumberland band of sundown towns and counties then continues across the Alabama line into the Sand Mountains, notorious in the 1930s and '40s

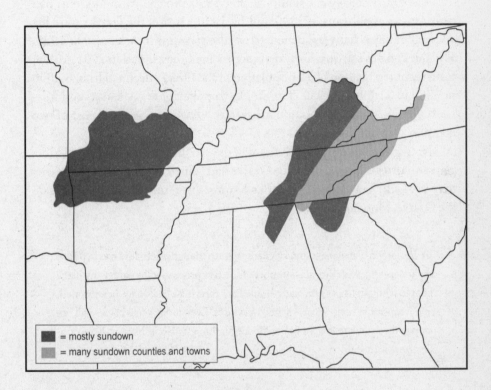

Map 3. Sundown Areas in the Nontraditional South

The lightly-shaded area denotes parts of Appalachia where some counties and towns went sundown, mostly after 1890. Heavily-shaded areas include a V-shaped region in north Georgia, the Cumberlands, and the Ozarks, where *most* counties and towns went sundown, again mainly after 1890.

for their sundown signs. Portfolio 15 shows a representation of such a sign from the 1930s. Historian Charles Martin told of an "old-timer," interviewed by one of his students, who used the usual sundown "problem" rhetoric: "We didn't have any racial problems back then. As long as they were off the mountain by sundown, there weren't any problems." [71]

The Ozarks also went sundown after 1890. No county in Missouri had zero African Americans in 1890, but by 1930, most of the Ozarks were lily white. The same thing happened across the state line in Arkansas. In 1923, William Pickens saw sundown signs across the Ozarks. And in 2001, Milton Rafferty noted that the black population of the Ozarks declined from 62,000 in 1860 to 31,000 by 1930. The sundown policy of the Arkansas and Missouri Ozarks spilled over into northeastern Oklahoma, leaving most of two counties all-white there. [72]

Noting sundown signs still extant in the 1970s, sociologist Gordon Morgan said African Americans in the Ozarks had coined a new term for the towns they marked: "gray towns." So far as I know, this term was not used outside the Ozarks. Morgan goes on:

> In the not too distant past some vigilante whites thought their duty was to police the towns and, with the tacit support of the law, proceeded to harass any black people who might pass through. Some cars carrying blacks have been stoned, and weapons have been brandished by whites. Even today some blacks will not stop in these gray towns for gas or food even though discrimination in the public places is forbidden.

In 2002, some African Americans who live near the Ozarks said they still avoid the region. [73]

The Great Retreat in the West

Table 1 points to the Great Retreat from every state in the Great Plains and Rocky Mountains. African Americans left most rural areas and retreated to a handful of cities with black population concentrations. Every state in the Great Plains and Rocky Mountains also saw a decline in overall black population percentages. States that had no centers of black population for African Americans to retreat to even saw declines in their absolute numbers of African Americans. The black population of North Dakota, for example, slid from

372 in 1890 to 243 in 1930. As a proportion of the population, blacks dropped from 0.2% in 1890 to a minuscule 0.03% by 1930. In South Dakota the decline was from 0.16% to 0.09%, in Montana from 1.13% to 0.23%. Six counties in Nebraska that had 20 to 50 African Americans each in 1890 had just 1 to 8 by 1930; at the same time, Omaha and Lincoln doubled in black population. Wyoming, the "equality state," had the largest proportion of African Americans in any of these states—1.52% in 1890, its year of statehood—but by 1930, blacks were only 0.55% of its population. Utah's blacks likewise decreased as a proportion of the population, and those who remained beat a retreat to Salt Lake and Weber (Ogden) Counties; by 1930, 88% of the state's African Americans lived in those two counties.

Again, these declines were hardly voluntary. We have already seen how, especially in the West, expulsions and prohibitions have been directed not only at African Americans, but also at Chinese Americans and sometimes others. Indeed, western locales established a bewildering variety of rules. Some towns in the West excluded Native Americans but not Chinese Americans. Minden and Gardnerville are adjoining towns south of Carson City, Nevada. In the 1950s, and probably for many years prior, a whistle sounded at 6 p.m., audible in both towns, to warn American Indians to be gone by sundown. William Jacobsen Jr., an anthropologist who lived in Gardnerville in 1955, says it worked: "Indians made themselves scarce." A Chinese American family didn't have to leave. On the other hand, Esmeralda County, two counties to the southeast, allowed black residents but not Chinese. Meanwhile Fallon, Nevada, had a big sign at the railroad depot that said "No Niggers or Japs allowed," and the newspaper in Rawhide, Nevada, bragged in 1908 that "Dagoes" from southern Europe, as well as African Americans, "have been kindly but friendly [sic] informed to move on."[74]

South Pasadena, a sundown suburb of Los Angeles, let in Native Americans while keeping out Mexican and Asian Americans. Historian Fred Rolater relates how Professor Manuel Servin at the University of Southern California became the first Mexican American to break the taboo, in about 1964. Servin bought the Loomis House, a historic mansion. South Pasadena thought he was Native American, which was OK; "what the city did not know," Rolater went on to point out, was that his family was from Mexico and had come to the United States in the 1920s. "Thus the anti-Mexican restrictive covenant was broken by a Ph.D. American Indian who happened to be Mexican."[75]

Other California towns also kept out Mexican Americans, including

Chester, a lumber mill town north of Sacramento, and Palos Verdes Estates, an elite oceanfront suburb of Los Angeles. Historian Margaret Marsh points to the irony of its sundown policy: "Palos Verdes excluded Mexican-Americans . . . from living in the estates, yet Mexican-inspired architecture was mandated in most of the area." According to the University of Colorado Latino/a Research and Policy Center, in the late 1930s Longmont, Colorado, sported signs saying "No Mexicans After Night." [76]

In 1907, whites in Bellingham, Washington, drove out its entire "Hindu" population—Sikhs, actually, numbering between 200 and 300—during three days of lawlessness. The chief of police, according to a pro-police account written years later, "recognized the universal demand of the whites that the brown men be expelled," so he had his men stand by while a mob did the work. "Like the Chinamen, who have never returned to Tacoma," the account concludes, "the Hindu has given Bellingham a wide berth since." The Bellingham newspaper editorialized against "the means employed," but expressed "general and intense satisfaction" with the results. "There can be no two sides to such a question," the editor concluded. "The Hindu is a detriment to the town, while the white man is a distinct advantage." [77]

Despite the West's patchwork policies—barring Native Americans but not Chinese here, Chinese Americans but not blacks there, Jews somewhere else—for the most part, as in other regions, racism has long been strongest toward African Americans. The West is dotted with independent sundown towns that kept out blacks—places such as Duncan and Scottsdale, Arizona; Murray, Utah; and Astoria, Oregon. California had just eight potential sundown counties but scores of confirmed or likely sundown towns and suburbs. Most suburbs of Los Angeles and San Francisco and most communities in Orange County were established as white-only.

Sundown Subregions and "Dead Lines"

We have seen that entire subregions of the United States, such as the Cumberlands, the Ozarks, and the suburbs of Los Angeles, went sundown—not every suburb of Los Angeles, not every county in the Ozarks or the Cumberlands, but enough to warrant the generalization. In several subregions of the United States, signs in rural areas, usually on major highways, announced "dead lines" beyond which blacks were not to go except at risk of life itself. In Mississippi County, Arkansas, for example, according to historian Michael Dougan, a "red line" that was originally a road surveyor's mark defined where blacks might not trespass beyond to the west. That line probably continued north into the Missouri Bootheel and west beyond Paragould, encompassing more than 2,000 square miles. In southern Illinois, African Americans were not permitted "to settle north of the Mobile & Ohio switch track. This has been a settled feeling for years," according to a 1924 newspaper report that described a series of attacks—arson, attempted murder, and dynamite—against blacks who tried to move north of that line and against a white farmer in Elco who hired them. Unconfirmed oral history in east Wisconsin holds that there was a sign outside Fond du Lac along Highway 41 warning that blacks were not welcome north of there. This sign sighting needs corroboration but is credible, because in addition to Fond du Lac itself and confirmed sundown towns Appleton and Oshkosh, all towns north of that point were overwhelmingly white.[78] The Arkansas and Illinois dead lines may still be in effect; as recently as 1992, a black friend said, "I can't go into that town," to reporter Jack Tichenor when he proposed buying a bag of charcoal after dark in Karnak, just north of the Illinois dead line. However, African Americans do live north of the Wisconsin line without difficulty today.[79]

From west to east, other confirmed sundown subregions—not just individual counties or towns—include:

- A 4,000-square-mile area southwest of Fort Worth, Texas, including Comanche, Hamilton, and Mills counties, where whites drove out African Americans in 1886
- A thick band of sundown counties and towns on both sides of the Iowa-Missouri border
- Virtually every town and city along the Illinois River, from its mouth at the Mississippi northeast almost to Chicago, except Peoria

Still other subregions need confirmation. More research is needed, everywhere.

The Great Retreat from Prime Real Estate

Another way of characterizing the distribution of intentionally white communities in the United States is by type rather than location. From the Great

Lakes, moving east to New England, then south to Florida, and then again in California and Oregon, we see the practice of keeping African Americans (and often Jews) off prime beauty spots such as islands, beaches, and coasts, and outside the city limits of oceanside towns. In mountain areas in the East, beginning in the late 1880s, many vacation destinations and retirement communities sprouted "Restricted" signs, meaning "white Gentiles only." Elegant seaside suburbs such as Manchester-by-the-Sea, Massachusetts, kept out all Jews and all African Americans except servants living in white residences. Long Island exemplified the process in microcosm: most of its beach communities kept blacks out, while the inside, the potato farm area, was interracial.[80]

Famous tourist spots such as Seaside Park, New Jersey, and Rehoboth Beach, Delaware, were for whites only. African Americans and "Moors," a local mixed-race people, worked in Rehoboth Beach but could not live there, according to Elizabeth Baxter, who resided in Rehoboth in the late 1930s; this was confirmed by an 84-year-old lifelong resident. Nor could Jews. Islands and beaches in the Carolinas and Georgia, including Wrightsville Beach, North Carolina, and Isle of Palms, South Carolina, were all-white into the 1990s. Florida is rimmed with sundown communities on both coasts. California had even more, especially clustered around Los Angeles and San Francisco. Some of these towns are elite, some multiclass, some working-class.[81]

Several Florida beach towns, such as Delray Beach, between Fort Lauderdale and West Palm Beach, kept out Jews but not African Americans. In 1959, the Anti-Defamation League of B'nai B'rith described Delray Beach as "one of the nation's most completely anti-Semitic communities." It quoted a leading Delray Beach realtor who proudly called it "the only city on the East Coast [of Florida] fully restricted to Gentiles both in buying and selling."[82] A longtime resident told me, "Mostly northerners lived there, not southerners, but they were just as prejudiced. They didn't want Delray Beach to become majority Jewish and garish like Miami Beach." At the time Delray Beach had 5,363 African Americans in its population of 12,230; in the North, rarely did a place keep out Jews while admitting African Americans. On the Pacific coast, La Jolla, California, legally part of San Diego but often thought of as an independent community with its own zip code, long kept out Jews, African Americans, and Mexican Americans. In 1925, the Parent-Teacher Associations asked the La Jolla Civic League to prevent "a Mexican Squatter" from occupying land he had leased in La Jolla. According to Leonard Valdez of Sacramento, La Jolla was still keeping out Mexican Americans in the 1960s.

Of course, Valdez noted, many retired naval officers lived in La Jolla, and "there were no Mexican naval officers." [83]

Almost All Suburbs Were Sundown Towns

Residential areas near cities are also valuable real estate, of course, owing to their proximity to jobs, cultural venues, up-to-date health care, and other big-city amenities. To a still greater extent than vacation areas, suburbs went all-white, beginning in about 1900. The so-called Progressive movement, beginning shortly thereafter, was for whites only. Among its tenets was the notion that the big city and its ward politics—dominated by immigrants and "the machine"—were "dirty." The answer was to move to the suburbs, leaving the dirt, vice, pollution—and African Americans—behind.

Across the United States, most suburbs came into existence well after the sundown town movement was already under way. In suburbia, excluding African Americans (and often Jews) became the rule, not the exception. As we saw in Mississippi and Alabama, even the traditional South was not exempt, developing its share of sundown suburbs, mostly after World War II.

Like beaches and resort towns, suburbs added another ground for exclusion—religion—that most independent towns ignored. Many and perhaps most suburbs of Boston, New York, Philadelphia, Chicago, Minneapolis, and Los Angeles, as well as smaller cities such as Harrisburg, Pennsylvania, kept out Jews for decades. Long Island was especially vicious. Some suburbs kept out Catholics.

Sundown suburbs continued to be developed rather recently, many between 1946 and 1968. The peak for independent sundown towns was probably reached around 1940. Between 1940 and 1968, a handful of independent towns went sundown, such as Vienna, Illinois, which burned out its black community in 1954, but African Americans successfully moved into a larger handful of sundown towns, such Portales, New Mexico, in about the same year. Thus the overall number of independent sundown towns dropped a bit after 1940. Not so for sundown suburbs. Until 1968, new all-white suburbs were forming much more rapidly than old sundown towns and suburbs were caving in. Thus 1968 might be the peak year for independent sundown towns and sundown suburbs combined. [84]

To supply an exact number of sundown towns in the United States is hard, partly because it depends on the definition of "town," but in many states outside the South, a majority of all towns [85] can probably be confirmed as sundown in 1968. [86] In all, I believe at least 3,000 and perhaps as many as 15,000 independent towns went sundown in the United States, mostly between 1890 and about 1930. Another 2,000 to 10,000 sundown suburbs formed a little later, between 1900 and 1968.[87] The range is broad because I could not and did not locate every sundown town in America; there are far too many. I have confirmed about 1,000 sundown towns and suburbs across the United States but have left many more unconfirmed.

Sundown Neighborhoods

White America's new craze for all-white residential areas extended also into central cities and inner suburbs. As we have seen, African American were too numerous to be driven from larger cities such as Chicago and Washington, D.C., or medium-sized ones such as Omaha or Tulsa, but after 1890, neighborhoods within cities and inner suburbs increasingly went all-white.

As a rule, American cities had not been very racially segregated in the nineteenth century. During the Nadir, that began to change. Cities and towns that did not expel their African Americans after 1890 concentrated them into a few neighborhoods. Residential segregation increased dramatically within northern cities between 1900 and 1960. Even in places far removed not only from the South but also from any large population of African Americans, blacks now found themselves unwelcome. Historian Howard Chudacoff describes the increasing residential segregation in Omaha:

> During the last decades of the 19th century Omaha housing was available to all who could meet the price, blacks included. . . . Beginning in 1902, however, the newspapers printed increasing numbers of housing advertisements specifying "for colored families." For other groups, more freedom of choice prevailed.

Roy Stannard Baker found residential segregation growing everywhere, including once-liberal Boston: "A strong prejudice exists against renting flats and houses in many white neighborhoods to colored people. The Negro in Boston, as in other cities, is building up 'quarters,' which he occupies to the increasing exclusion of other classes[88] of people."[89]

The Index of Dissimilarity (D) provides a common measure of the degree of residential segregation within a metropolitan area.[90] When $D = 0$, integration is perfect: every census tract has exactly the same racial composition as every other census tract. 100 represents complete apartheid: not one black in any white area, not one white in any black area. For values between 0 and 100, D tells the percentage of the smaller group—usually African Americans—that would have to move from disproportionately black areas to white areas to achieve a completely neutral distribution of both races. In 1860, the average northern city had a D of 45.7—only moderately segregated. If 45.7% of the blacks in an average city moved to predominantly white neighborhoods, the city would be perfectly integrated. Reynolds Farley and William Frey, premier researchers on residential segregation, point out that until about 1900, "in northern cities, some blacks shared neighborhoods with poor immigrants from Europe." Even middle-class areas were interracial: "Tiny cadres of highly educated blacks lived among whites in prosperous neighborhoods." Southern cities were even less segregated spatially, with an average D of 29.0. To some degree, especially in the South, these low D's reflected the age-old pattern of servant housing near upper-class white housing. Even so, the low indexes reflected a lack of residential racial segregation, especially in working-class areas.[91]

After 1900, hostility ranging from shunning to violence forced the involuntary retrenchment of African Americans from dispersed housing in many parts of the city to concentration in inner-city ghettoes—an intracity manifestation of the Great Retreat. By 1910, northern cities averaged 59.2 and southern cities 38.3 on the Index of Dissimilarity. Even larger increases characterized the next few decades. By 1920, D was above 80 in most northern U.S. cities, and the South was catching up. Northern cities averaged 89.2 in 1940, southern cities 81.0. By 1960, the average northern city held at 85.6, while the average southern city rose to 91.9.[92] These are astonishing levels, considering that the end of the scale, 100, means not one black in any white neighborhood and not one white in any black neighborhood.

Creating All-Black Towns

During the Nadir, African Americans were hardly passive victims. They thrashed about, trying tactic after tactic to deal with America's increasing racism. One was the development of all-black towns. It is a matter of semantics, I suppose, whether these towns were an alternative to the Great Retreat or part of it. Certainly they were founded at precisely the same time.

Some commentators have interpreted the black-town movement as a giving up on white America. On the contrary, black towns such as Nicodemus, Kansas; Boley, Oklahoma; and Mound Bayou, Mississippi, emulated white towns. Indeed, their initial development was marked by a sense of self-respect and competition: they wanted to outdo white towns. They also hoped to provide employment and political opportunities not available elsewhere. Black towns ran their own post offices, which therefore hired African Americans, even when the Woodrow Wilson administration was shutting blacks out of this work. Black towns ran their own precincts, which therefore let African Americans vote, even as the outside society was shutting blacks out of politics.

To be sure, black towns were founded in a difficult, even dangerous period. The movement began in reply to the end of Reconstruction in the South, when African Americans were no longer voting freely and lynchings were increasing. In 1879, African Americans began an exodus from Mississippi and Louisiana to Indian Territory and Kansas, trying to find freedom and peace. In 1887, hoping to avoid the worst of the racist storm, African Americans founded Mound Bayou in former swampland in the Mississippi Delta. In 1904, African Americans in Indian Territory founded Boley. Both towns grew rapidly, fueled by a wave of optimism similar to that at the end of the Civil War, tinged this time with desperation. By 1908, Boley had 2,500 residents, two banks, two cotton gins, a newspaper, a hotel, and a college, the Creek-Seminole College and Agriculture Institute. Briefly Boley competed with Okemah, Weleetka, and Henryetta, nearby white-majority towns, for economic and political influence in the area.[93]

Unfortunately, the history of Boley and its neighboring towns shows that black towns offered no real solution to the increasing racism of the Nadir. Gradually Boley's residents themselves realized they were to have no real chance at social, economic, or political rights, owing to forces outside their town and beyond their control. In 1907, whites merged Indian Territory into the new state of Oklahoma. Democrats took over the state and passed vicious segregation laws modeled on Mississippi's 1890 constitution. Although the research has yet to be done by historians and sociologists in Oklahoma, I believe it will show that a wave of small expulsions swept through many Oklahoma towns shortly after statehood, as white Democrats reveled in their newly realized power over African and Native Americans.

Boley is located in Okfuskee County. Okemah, the county seat, had been founded as a sundown town in 1902. From time to time African Americans moved in, only to face violent opposition. In January 1907, for example, whites dynamited the homes of the only two black families in town.[94] Later that year, Okemah businessmen leased a building and set up a hotel for African Americans who traded with the local merchants or had to attend court and could not always get back to Boley by sundown. By April 1908 it was doing a brisk business, which ended when other whites placed a heavy charge of dynamite under the front wall of the hotel. "The building was badly damaged," wrote Okemah resident W. L. Payne. "Farmers living eight miles from Okemah were aroused by the terrific blast. This brought about a quick reduction in the Negro population of Okemah."[95]

Henryetta, the next town to the east, went sundown in December 1907. According to the *History of Okmulgee County,* "A number of black families— perhaps as many as 200 people—lived in one area of Henryetta"; just south of town lived another 30 or 40 black miners and their families. On Christmas Eve, James Gordon, African American, tried to rent a rig from Albert Bates, white, who owned a livery stable. Bates refused, an altercation followed, and Gordon shot him. A posse soon caught Gordon a mile east of town and brought him to the jail. Whites "were incensed. They surrounded the jail, battered down the door, smashed the jail lock with a sledge hammer, and dragged Gordon across the street to a telephone pole," where they "hanged him and riddled his body with bullets." All the next day, Christmas Day, "there were rumors of black uprisings," according to the county history:

> The talk on the street was that "no more negroes will be allowed to domicile in Henryetta." . . . Within a day or two, the whites rallied together with guns, rocks, bricks, "anything and everything" and ran the other black families out of town. "We didn't care where they went and don't know," said one irate resident. From then on, Henryetta was off-limits to blacks except for business during the day.[96]

Then Democrats eliminated Boley as a voting precinct and forced citizens of Boley to vote in a smaller town twelve miles away. Boley voters turned out in droves and compelled the whites running that precinct to let them cast ballots, which Democrats then didn't include in countywide tallies anyway. In 1910, Democrats amended the Oklahoma constitution with a "grandfather clause" that set up literacy requirements to keep African Americans from voting; whites were exempt so long as their ancestors could vote in 1861. Blacks' grandfathers, being slaves then, could not vote, so the combination took away the ballot from African Americans while granting it to European Americans.[97]

Residents of Boley still hoped they could just mind their own business and run their own affairs, but whites weren't satisfied with merely excluding African Americans from voting. In Bittle and Geis's words, "Not only would all avenues of political expression be cut off, but all avenues of social and economic expression as well." White neighbors set up Farmers' Commercial Clubs,

> the express purpose of which was to drive the Negro farmers from the area and to replace them with white farmers. Pacts were drawn up between whites in which each agreed to withhold employment from Negroes. . . . With each dreadful development, the Negroes attempted to reorganize their ethic for yet another time. But this reorientation became patently vapid, and the Negro community simply relented in the face of white hostility.

In 1911, Okemah residents lynched a mother and son who lived in the black community outside Boley (Portfolio 11), showing that a black town provided no safe harbor from white vigilante "justice." The drop in cotton prices in 1913 finished the job. Now Boley started to lose population. "The economic and political setbacks added up to almost total disillusionment on the part of the Okfuskee County Negroes. . . . There would be no growing respect and admiration from white neighbors and no industrial and agricultural prosperity." Boley still holds its annual celebration, but it became a shell of its former self. Its pariah status, conferred by the all-white towns nearby, sapped its morale.[98]

Black Townships

Sprinkled about the United States, often located at the edge of sundown towns or a few miles away, are other, smaller black communities, most of which never incorporated, many with dirt roads, off the beaten path. They are the flip side of sundown towns—places to which the excluded have retreated to live, yet close enough to nearby white towns to work. I call them "townships" because some of them resemble South Africa's black townships, those gatherings of shacks built by squatters that supply maids for Johannesburg's white households and janitors for its industries. Like Thokoza and Soweto, in America often these were haphazard gatherings of ramshackle houses, many of which were not, until recently, served by amenities such as city water.[99] Some still are not.

If even independent black towns succumbed to the demoralizing effect the increased racism of the Nadir had on African Americans nationally, townships showed much less heritage of black pride. They too offered some refuge from the racist storm, but they never made any pretense of providing a solution to America's racial inequality. The little area that housed African American adjoining Eugene, Oregon, during World War II was dubbed "Tent City" because its "houses" consisted of tents pitched over wooden frameworks on wooden floors.[100] To some degree, these communities resemble reservations—places to which whites restricted African Americans, whose labor they desired but whose presence they did not want. Their residents knew it.

Chevy Chase Heights was an unincorporated community located just north of the town of Indiana in western Pennsylvania. In 1960, when college student Ralph Stone studied Chevy Chase Heights, he elicited only scorn when he asked a clerk at the Indiana Chamber of Commerce for information on the community. "Who in the world would want to know that?" she replied. Asked if she at least had population figures for the community, she replied, "Nobody knows. If you want to know, go out and count them." Chevy Chase residents repeatedly petitioned Indiana for annexation so that they could have street lights, paved streets, and city sewage lines, and the settlement, "for geographical reasons, should be part of the borough," according to Stone. But Indiana "wants nothing to do with Chevy Chase," he concluded. Indeed, Indiana made this clear long before 1960: local historian Clarence Stephenson quotes a Works Progress Administration source telling that "the [black] families that formerly lived in the borough of Indiana were asked by the borough council to locate in Chevy Chase." By 1960, according to Stone, 20 African Americans remained in Indiana and about 577 lived in Chevy Chase Heights.[101]

Even their names sometimes imply the racism that was their reason for being. For years "The Colony" was the name used by blacks as well as whites for the mostly African American community south of Cullman, Alabama. A librarian in Cullman explained, "The only full-time African American residents of the entire county through most of its history have lived in a tiny community called 'The Colony' which is roughly twenty miles south of the city. . . . 'The Colony' was incorporated as 'Colony' in 1980." African Americans who worked as maids and handymen commuted into Cullman in the mid-1950s by carpools. The Colony had an elementary school, but before Cullman's schools desegregated in 1970, African Americans who wanted to go to high school had go to another county. Colp, Illinois, a majority-black hamlet 1 mile west of Herrin and 3 miles north of Carterville, began as #9 Mine, a coal mine that employed African American miners. White miners called it "Nigger Nine." Understandably taking offense, citizens of #9 Mine incorporated in 1915 as Colp, named for John Colp, the mine owner who employed them. But Herrin residents think Colp is short for "colored people" and thus mounts no challenge to white sensibilities. Now that mining has wound down, Colp residents work in Herrin, but for years Herrin residents informally threatened them with death if they remained overnight, and they could not set foot in nearby Carterville even during the daytime. Residents of Stump Town, a small African American community in western Illinois, worked in Warsaw but had to be out of there by nightfall. Residents of other sundown towns across the Midwest and border states simply called the little black townships near them "Niggertown," while its African American residents struggled to have them known by more specific and less demeaning terms, including "Little Africa" in southern Illinois.[102]

Metropolitan areas, too, have their black townships. Suburban Long Island alone has thirteen.[103] For that matter, many residents of sundown suburbs have long relied on maids and gardeners who commute from inner-city ghettoes, which are analogous to black townships. Some suburban black settlements date back to the nineteenth century.[104] Others grew after World War II, when white suburbs likewise exploded. Typically black townships supplied workers for nearby suburbs that wanted maids and gardeners but didn't want African Americans to spend the night. Often they were located in floodplains or next to railroad tracks just outside the city limits of the nearest suburb. In 1966, sociologists Leonard Blumberg and Michael Lalli identified sixty of these communities, which they called "little ghettoes . . . in the suburbs." Most of these communities were unincorporated or did not enforce their zoning ordinances and building codes, which allowed African Americans to build their own homes, keep chickens and even pigs, and thus create rural pockets in urban areas. Over time, however, as blacks were not allowed to live in incorporated suburbs, the stigmatized nature of the townships as "permitted locations for a negatively valued population," to use Blumberg and Lalli's formulation, became apparent to all. Geographer Harold Rose calls them "black colonies in the metropolitan ring."[105]

Not only African Americans but also other "deviants" were often confined to these black townships. In the 1950s and '60s, Colp had a regionally famous house of prostitution; it still has a thriving bar.[106] As early as the 1970s, the Chevy Chase Heights Community Center hosted monthly gay dances. In the 1960s, the Elks Club and Sadler's Bar in Chevy Chase Heights were perhaps the only places in Indiana County where whites and blacks might socialize and even dance together. Indeed, *within* black towns and townships, race relations were often good. "In Chevy Chase a man is treated as a man regardless of color," said Fred Johnson, black Elks Club member in 1960. "In Indiana a white man is treated as a man, but a colored man is treated as an animal." Residents of sundown towns usually put down whites who socialized or lived in nearby "black" townships as "white trash." At the same time, whites in sundown towns often drove to nearby black townships to buy alcohol during Prohibition.[107] For decades Locke, a Chinese township in California founded in 1915, supplied gambling, prostitution, and opium to residents of Sacramento. Today, locations in black inner-city neighborhoods play the same role for whites from sundown suburbs seeking illegal drugs.[108]

Unincorporated townships such as Stump Town and Chevy Chase Heights—and black ghettoes, for that matter—have no police forces of their own. White sheriffs and police chiefs often wink at deviant or illegal behavior in black townships, as it fulfills three functions at once in the white community. It relieves the demand for the deviance, which usually involves victimless "crimes" like drinking, gambling, buying drugs, and buying sex. It avoids arousing the forces of priggery because the behavior does not take place in neighborhoods they care about, hence is not salient. And it further stigmatizes both the black township and African Americans in general.

Alternatives to the Great Retreat

The Great Retreat to the larger cities of the North and West and to black towns and townships was not African Americans' only response to the wave of increasing white hostility they met during the Nadir—but there was no good answer. Following Booker T. Washington's advice to "cast down your buckets where you are" and seek only economic advancement, forgoing political and social rights, didn't work; white southerners sometimes lynched successful black businessmen and farmers simply because they were successful. Following the counsel of W. E. B. DuBois and pursuing voting rights and full citizenship led to such fiascoes as the Ocoee, Florida, riot, described in Chapter 7, in which whites drove out the entire black population and converted Ocoee to a sundown town.

We have seen that moving to small towns in the North became difficult as more and more of them went sundown. Emigrating to Indian Territory, which at first promised a more tolerant multiracial milieu, led to the overt racism of

Oklahoma after 1907, including sundown towns such as Okemah and Henryetta. Going farther west didn't work either; an African American in Denver lamented in 1910 that what he called "the onslaught" against the race had reached Colorado, even though "the Mexican, Japanese, Chinese, and all other races are given a chance." Giving up hope for America, the author wrote, "We are leaving in great numbers to the far northwest, taking up claims in Canada." But Canada offered no real refuge; Portfolio 17 shows that it considered closing its doors to blacks entirely. African Americans in Boley and in many interracial towns joined the back-to-Africa movements organized by Chief Sam and Marcus Garvey. The popularity of these movements did not derive from any developments in Africa but was another aspect of the Great Retreat, prompted by the white racism exemplified in the sundown town crusade. The movements organized by both Sam and Garvey ended in disarray, partly because they expressed pride and despair more than actual intentions to emigrate.[109]

The Great Retreat Was No Solution

We have seen that forming black towns and townships offered only partial relief. So did moving to large cities, which increasingly segregated their African American residents into constricted ghettos and marginal occupations. Despair seemed to be the only answer to the hatred of the Nadir. Still relevant were the old slave spirituals such as "Nobody Knows the Trouble I've Seen."

Certainly the Great Retreat did not improve race relations. Regardless of how sundown towns were created, the whites within them only became more racist. They almost had to, to rationalize having forced or kept nonwhites out. Writing about Omaha, Howard Chudacoff points out another reason: because African Americans increasingly lived in separate neighborhoods, whites no longer had the benefit of knowing them individually, so they fell back on thinking stereotypically about them as a group. "The lack of familiarity bred suspicion and resentment which burst during the riot of 1919."[110]

Chudacoff concludes, "Clearly, the experience of Negroes resembled those of no other ethnic group." Every white ethnic group experienced and even chose residential concentration during their initial immigration to the United States. Thereafter, as the years passed and they became more Americanized, their residential concentration decreased—precisely when it was rising for African Americans. As the years passed, African Americans found themselves more and more isolated—increasingly barred from towns, suburbs, and neighborhoods.[111]

How did this happen? How were sundown towns (and counties and neighborhoods) created? What were the mechanisms by which so many towns became all-white or, in the case of suburbs, created themselves that way? The next chapter tries to answer these questions.

4

How Sundown Towns Were Created

Negro Driven Away
The Last One Leaves Decatur, Ind., Owing to Threats Made

The last Negro has left Decatur, Ind. His departure was caused by the anti-Negro feeling. About a month ago a mob of 50 men drove out all the Negroes who were then making that city their home. Since that time the feeling against the Negro race has been intense, so much so that an Anti-Negro Society was organized.

The colored man who has just left came about three weeks ago, and since that time received many threatening letters. When he appeared on the streets he was insulted and jeered at. An attack was threatened. . . .

The anti-negroites declare that as Decatur is now cleared of Negroes they will keep it so, and the importation of any more will undoubtedly result in serious trouble.

— *New York Times,* July 14, 1902[1]

A FINE HISTORY by Jean Swaim of Cedar County, Missouri, provides a detailed example of the process that took place in many of the counties summarized in Table 1 of the previous chapter. Cedar County is located between Kansas City and Springfield, Missouri. African Americans had lived in the county since before the Civil War, originally as slaves. In the 1870s, a black community grew up within Stockton, the county seat, including a school, candy store, and "a park with a popular croquet court, where white Stockton men often spent their Sunday afternoons competing in tournaments." Some African Americans worked as domestic help, others at a local brickyard. By 1875, whites and blacks had organized the Stockton Colored School, which eventually had as many as 43 students. A newspaper account from August 1899 shows interracial cooperation: "About 1,500 attended colored people's picnic here. Order was good except for a few drunken whites. Stockton won the ball game from Greenfield, 20-1. Greenfield's colored band was a big attraction." African Americans also lived elsewhere in the county, including "Little Africa" near Humansville in the northeastern corner. Forty families lived there, with a church, school, and store. They held an annual picnic on the Fourth of July to which whites were invited and had a baseball team with a white coach.[2]

Then something bad happened, something that the local histories don't identify and that has been lost even to oral history. As another local historian, born in the county in the 1920s, put it, "It's just a dark history that nobody talks about," speaking of the event or chain of events that ended Cedar County's racial harmony.[3] Around 1900, the county's black population declined precipitously, from 127 (in 1890) to 45. Whatever prompted the initial decline, we do know why it continued: Cedar County was becoming a sundown county. By 1910, only thirteen African Americans lived in the county, and by 1930, just one. Swaim refers to "many shameful incidents" in which "visiting ball teams, travelers, and even laborers were . . . told to be out of town by night. Blacks could find haven in Greenfield," the seat of the next county to the south. She tells of a black bricklayer whose work attracted admiring crowds: "Not only was he paving El Dorado Springs's Main Street in perfect herringbone pattern as fast as an assistant could toss him bricks, but he sang as he worked and moved in rhythm to his song." Nevertheless, he "had to find a place out of town at night." "In Stockton, prejudice was still rampant in the late 1960s," Swaim continues, "as black workmen constructing the Stockton Dam were provided segregated and inferior housing west of town. Their visiting wives cooked for them." Is Cedar County still sundown today? Swaim writes, "In the 1990s few blacks are seen in Cedar County." But the 2000 census counted 44 African Americans. One black couple lives in El Dorado Springs and seems to get along all right. Nevertheless, Cedar County in 2005 has yet to reach the level of black population and interracial cooperation that it showed in the 1890s.[4]

Swaim's fine account, summarized above, provides the texture of the Great Retreat from one Missouri county, but neither Swaim nor the other historian quite say how it all began. The initial "how" in Cedar County may be lost to history by this point. But in many other places, we do know how counties and towns went sundown, or how they were created that way in the first place. This chapter examines the variety of methods by which town after town across America excluded African Americans, mostly after 1890. We begin with violence because it was the most important. Moreover, threat of violent force underlies many of the "softer" methods: ordinance, informal actions by police and public officials, freezing out blacks from social interaction and from institutions such as schools and churches, buying them out, and other forms of bad behavior by white residents of the town. By dint of these methods, independent sundown towns were created, mostly between 1890 and 1930. Sundown suburbs were created a little later, mostly between 1900 and 1968, by a panoply of methods, among which violence and intimidation were also prominent.

Creating Sundown Towns by Violence

Often white residents achieved their goal abruptly, even in the middle of the night. *In town after town in the United States, especially between 1890 and the 1930s, whites forced out their African American neighbors violently, as they had the Chinese in the West.* Decatur, in northeastern Indiana, went sundown in 1902, as told in the excerpt above from the *New York Times*. Adams County, of which Decatur is the county seat, wound up without a single black household; a century later, it still had only five. Decatur exemplifies a widespread phenomenon: little riots, most of which have never been written about, even by local historians. These are cases of what Donald Horowitz calls "the deadly ethnic riot." He cites examples from India, Kyrgyztan, Malaysia, Nigeria, and other countries, and defines the form as:

> an intense, sudden, though not necessarily wholly unplanned, lethal attack by civilian members of one ethnic group on civilian members of another ethnic group, the victims chosen because of their group membership. . . . Members of one ethnic group search out members of another. The search is conducted with considerable care, for this is violence directed against an identifiable target group.[5]

Towns with successful riots wound up all-white, of course, or almost so, and therefore had an ideological interest in suppressing any memory of a black population in the first place, let alone of an unseemly riot that drove them out.[6]

Whites also tried to "cleanse" at least fifteen larger cities of their more substantial nonwhite populations: Denver (of Chinese) in 1880; Seattle (of Chinese) in 1886; Akron in 1900; Evansville, Indiana, and Joplin, Missouri, in 1903; Springfield, Ohio, in 1904, 1906, and again in 1908; Springfield, Missouri, in 1906; Springfield, Illinois, in 1908; Youngstown, Ohio, and East St. Louis, Illinois, in 1917; Omaha and Knoxville in 1919; Tulsa in 1921; Johnstown, Pennsylvania, in 1923; and Lincoln, Nebraska, in 1929. (Portfolio

10 shows the attempt in Tulsa.) They failed, mainly because the task would have taken three or four days, giving their governors time not only to call out their state's national guard but also to realize they would get considerable criticism—and so would their state—if they failed to act.

Some of these larger riots have received some attention, including books and historical markers. Since they were unsuccessful—in that they failed to drive out all African Americans—they have left fuller records of the process, because interracial communities have no need to deny that they had once had a black population. As well, they have black populations with their own collective memories. Indeed, in Tulsa, an ongoing controversy concerns reparations. But most of the little riots have gone entirely overlooked, and as a result, the pattern of widespread "ethnic cleansings," of which these failed large attempts represent the tip of the iceberg, is not generally understood. Moreover, even when the cleansings were incomplete, they made a profound impact upon surrounding towns, often inspiring satellite riots.

Consider the 1903 attack on the black community in Joplin. As was often the case, it started with an act of violence against one white person, in this case the murder of a police officer. There was little doubt that the assailant was a black tramp named Thomas Gilyard, who was quickly taken into custody. Several hundred white people then gathered outside the jail, broke through the wall, and lynched him, after a tug-of-war with other whites who tried to stop it. Then the mob went through black neighborhoods, attacking African Americans, burning their homes, and cutting firemen's hoses so they couldn't intervene. Half of Joplin's 770 African American residents fled for their lives. Joplin was large enough that the mob could not drive all African Americans from the city, but the results are still plain: in 2000 Joplin had a lower African American population proportion—just 2.7%—than it did in 1902. Moreover, this riot, along with several others in Missouri and Arkansas, helped foment an ideology of ethnic cleansing that made most of the Ozark Plateau a sundown region by 1920.[7]

Another unsuccessful cleansing—in Springfield, Illinois—had a still greater impact. In 1908, residents of Springfield acted on their desire to have an all-white city. A white woman, Mabel Hallam, claimed George Richardson, an African American, had raped her. Police jailed him, whereupon a mob gathered at the county jail to lynch him, along with another black prisoner accused of murder. The sheriff borrowed an automobile from businessman Harry Loper, however, and managed to get both prisoners safely out of town. Angry at being foiled, the mob destroyed Loper's restaurant and then turned its rage on the African American community in general. According to Roberta

Senechal, whose book is the standard source on the riot, "During two days of violence, white rioters gutted the capitol's black business district, left blocks of black homes in smoldering ruins, and lynched two innocent black men," Scott Burton and William Donnegan. "The rioters' ultimate goal seemingly was to drive away all of Springfield's blacks," Senechal concluded. The task was simply too large, however, since Springfield in 1908 had about 3,100 African Americans in a total population of 48,000.[8] Nevertheless, some 2,000 did flee the city. Only the belated arrival of the Illinois state militia kept the mob from finishing the job. Springfield being the capital, the state government simply could not ignore this riot.[9]

The Springfield riot was famous briefly throughout the world, not because it was unusual, which it was not, but because it happened in Abraham Lincoln's hometown.[10] Springfield's history encapsulates America's downward course in race relations from the Civil War to the Nadir. When Lincoln's funeral train brought his body back to Springfield for burial in 1865, a regiment of black troops led the procession to the state capitol. Thousands of African Americans "had journeyed for days in order to be in Springfield at the funeral," according to an officer in the military escort for Lincoln's body. Afterward, some of them stayed on to live in the city. Now the townspeople of the Great Emancipator were trying to expel them all. "Abe Lincoln brought them to Springfield and we will drive them out!" shouted members of the mob.[11]

After the riot, Hallam admitted she made up the story about being raped, to cover up an affair she was having. Nevertheless, most Springfield residents showed no regret, except about failing to drive every last black person from the city. The tree from which the mob hanged Scott Burton, a black barber, was hacked to pieces to make souvenirs of the occasion. After the riot, some employers fired their black employees, and many local shopkeepers now refused to serve African Americans. Later, 107 people were charged with crimes, but the only person sentenced was a man convicted of petty theft for stealing a sword from a National Guardsman. No one was ever convicted for murder, arson, or any other crime against an African American.[12]

The Springfield riot stands as a prototype for the many smaller riots that left communities all-white between 1890 and 1940, most of which have never been written about by any historian. Indeed, the Springfield riot itself spawned a host of imitators: whites shouted "Give 'em Springfield!" during attacks on African Americans as far away as Alton, Illinois; Evansville, Indiana; St. Louis, Missouri; and the Cumberland Plateau in Kentucky and Tennessee. Closer to home, the *Illinois State Register* reported, "At Auburn, Thayer, Virden, Girard, Pawnee, Spaulding, Buffalo, Riverton, Pana, Edinburg, Taylorville, Pleasant Plains, and a score of other places in central Illinois a Negro is an unwelcome visitor and is soon informed he must not remain in the town." [13] Some of these towns, such as Virden and Pana, were sundown towns before the Springfield riot; their exclusion policies had merely become newsworthy owing to the riot. Others, such as Buffalo and Pleasant Plains, excluded African Americans in its aftermath. Neither the local, county, state, or federal governments ever brought anyone to justice for any of these expulsions from smaller towns. Buffalo, a little town twelve miles east of Springfield, became all-white on August 17, 1908, two days after the National Guard ended the Springfield riot. Not to be outdone by Springfield, whites in Buffalo posted the following ultimatum at the train station:

> All niggers are warned out of town by Monday, 12 m. sharp.
> Buffalo Sharp Shooters

Its black population fled, and since then Buffalo has been all-white. Today some whites commute from Buffalo to Springfield, because they feel Springfield is too black. Springfield was 15% African American in 2000. [14]

In addition to the small-town disturbances around Springfield in 1908, at least a score of other towns in Illinois alone became sundown through violence. Whites in Romeoville, in northeastern Illinois, expelled all the town's African Americans in June 1893 in a pitched battle in which eight people were killed. Other violent expulsions include Beardstown at an unknown date, East Alton and Spring Valley in 1895, [15] Virden in 1898, Pana in 1899, Carterville in 1901, [16] Eldorado in 1902, Anna-Jonesboro in 1909, West Frankfort in 1920, probably Pinckneyville in 1927 or 1928, and Vienna in 1954. Additional possible violent expulsions in Illinois that I have not confirmed include Newman back around 1879, Lacon and Toluca between 1898 and 1910, Granite City in 1903, Coal City at some undetermined date, and Zeigler by mine explosion in 1905. [17]

A series of at least six race riots in the Ozarks, along with smaller undocumented expulsions, led to the almost total whiteness of most Ozark counties, which continues to this day. In 1894, Monett, Missouri, started the chain of racial violence. As happened so often, it began with a lynching. Ulysses Hayden, an African American, was taken from police custody and hanged from a telephone pole, although Murray Bishoff, an authority on Monett, believes him innocent of the murder of the young white man for which he was hanged. After the lynching, whites forced all African Americans to leave Monett. Pierce City, just six miles west, followed suit in 1901. Again, a crime of violence had been perpetrated upon a white person, and again, after lynching the alleged perpetrator, the mob then turned on the black community, about 10% of the town's population, and drove them out.[18] In the process, members of the mob set fire to several homes, incinerating at least two African Americans inside. Portfolio 3 shows one of the destroyed residences. Some African Americans fled to Joplin, the nearest city, but in 1903 whites rioted there. Three years later, whites in Harrison, Arkansas, expelled most of their African Americans, and in 1909, they finished the job. In 1906, whites in Springfield, Missouri, staged a triple lynching they called an "Easter Offering."[19]

No one was ever convicted in any of these riots, which sent a message that violence against African Americans would not be punished in the Ozarks. On the contrary, it was celebrated. In Springfield, for example,

> souvenir hunters sifted through the smoldering ashes looking for bits of bone, charred flesh, and buttons to carry away with them in order to commemorate the event. Local drugstores and soda parlors sold postcards containing photo- graphs of the lynching, and one enterprising businessman . . . [had] medals struck commemorating the lynching. One side of the medal read "Easter Offer- ing," and the other side, "Souvenir of the hanging of 3 niggers, Springfield, Mis- souri, April 15, 1906."[20]

The immediate effect was a contagion of ethnic cleansing that drove African Americans from nearby towns such as Cotter, Arkansas. Sociologist Gordon Morgan wrote, "It is entirely possible that the trouble that was expe- rienced in Boone County [Harrison] affected the black populations in sur- rounding counties. The census shows precipitous drops in black numbers in the 1900–1910 decade in Carroll and Madison counties, both of which adjoin Boone."[21]

Elsewhere in the United States, I have been able to confirm mini-riots that forced out the black populations from at least 30 other towns, including Myakka City, Florida; Spruce Pine, North Carolina; Wehrum, Pennsylvania; Ravenna, Kentucky; Greensburg, Indiana; St. Genevieve, Missouri; and North Platte, Nebraska.[22] Many of these mini-riots in turn spurred whites in nearby towns to have their own, thus provoking small waves of expulsions.

Creating Sundown Towns by Threat

Sometimes just the threat of violence sufficed, especially where whites were many and blacks few, as in Buffalo. For that matter, because the historical record is incomplete, we cannot always know when violence or "mere" threat of violence forced a town's African Americans to leave. Most mass departures were probably forced by at least the threat of violence—why else would everyone leave at once?[23] Sometimes expulsions were more gradual, taking several years and requiring repeated threats or acts of violence.

When one member of the black community was lynched, all African Americans took that as a threat to their continued well-being. Often they were right. Frank Quillen, whose 1913 book *The Color Line in Ohio* stands as an oasis of honest scholarship during the arid Nadir period, observed that after a lynching, such as in Akron, Galion, and Urbana, Ohio, "I found the prejudice much stronger than it was before the lynching, and the Negroes fewer in number." A lynching by definition is a public murder. Those who carry it out do not bother to act in private, since they believe the community will support them. Thus a lynching becomes a community event in which all whites participate, at least vicariously, because the entire white community decides not to punish the perpetrators. After such an event, whites grew more likely to engage in such everyday practices as forcing African Americans from jobs like postal carrier or locomotive fireman, as well as from entire communities.[24]

The increasing frequency of mass "spectacle lynchings," in particular, played a major role in the spread of sundown towns. These events, often announced in advance, drew hundreds and even thousands of onlookers. Typically in their aftermath, not only was no one brought to justice, but also whites reveled in the brutality, selling fingers and bits of the victim's flesh as souvenirs and making postcards of photos of the event to send to friends across the country. Such events, reasonably enough, convinced African Americans in many towns that they were no longer safe. Chapter 7 tells how a spectacle lynching in Maryville, Missouri, not only caused African Americans to flee that town in 1931, but also led to their departure from neighboring counties.[25]

Mena, Arkansas, had a small African American population until February 20, 1901, when "Nigger Pete" was lynched. Pete was "considered by many locals to be insane," according to a 1986 article based on newspaper accounts of the time. He had gotten into "a fracas" with a twelve-year-old white girl, "knocking her down, and injuring her quite badly. Later in the evening Pete was arrested and placed in jail 'as has often been done before in similar offenses.' The episode flashed across town and it soon created strong feelings against the Negro." Whites then lynched him: they shot him, fractured his skull, and cut his throat. No one was ever apprehended for his death. According to an article written in 1980, "The black folks began to leave Polk County after the 'Nigger Pete' lynching." The county's African American population,

172 at one point, dropped to 12 in the aftermath, then slowly dwindled to zero as the remaining few died or moved away. Does this qualify as a violent expulsion? The African Americans obviously felt threatened. They also knew that two years earlier whites had posted notices around Mena warning blacks to leave. On that occasion other whites, including the mayor and newspaper editor, denounced the threat, but it had to have been unsettling nonetheless. Moreover, the editor had said then, "The number of Negro citizens in Mena is very small and as a whole exceeding well behaved. As long as these facts remain true they have their rights as citizens and the city officials will take any necessary steps to protect them." Pete's action, given whites' penchant for holding the entire African American community responsible for the misstep of any individual, threatened the premise undergirding white forbearance and prompted the expulsion. According to Shirley Manning, Mena historian:

> My father said he was only a boy of 5–7 (born in 1897) when the people of Polk
> County ran all the blacks out of town, and as they left from the race track, . . .
> white people set the wagons on fire. My dad died when I was 10, but I remember the story, and my much older brother has told it to me, also.

So in Mena, at least, threat of violence crossed over into actual attack.[26]

Many other towns saw their African American populations leave suddenly after one member of the group was lynched. On February 10, 1918, for example, whites in Estill Springs, Tennessee, lynched G. W. Lych, an African American minister. Two days later, in a spectacle lynching, they burned another African American alive before 1,500 spectators; "black residents of the community were forced to watch," according to Stewart Tolnay and E. M. Beck. "After the incident the black population of Estill Spring[s] quickly disappeared." The lynching of an African American by whites from Toluca and Lacon, north of Peoria, Illinois, in 1898 probably led to the exodus of African Americans from those towns.[27]

The Role of the Ku Klux Klan

The rise of the KKK after 1915—the so-called second Klan—often amounted to an implicit threat to blacks in largely white communities. In many towns across the North, from Maine to Illinois to Oregon, Klan rallies in the 1920s drew more people than any assemblages before or since. (See Portfolio 21 and 22.) On August 20, 1923, for example, 8,500 members of the Ku Klux Klan met two miles east of West Frankfort, Illinois—a gathering equal to the town's entire population at the time—and inducted 400 new members. A 1925 Klan rally near Montpelier, Vermont, drew nearly 10,000, almost twice that city's population. Such huge gatherings gave whites a sense of power, a feeling that they could do whatever they wanted to African Americans, and sometimes to Jews and Catholics as well. West Frankfort was already a sundown town, but in towns with black residents, these monster demonstrations had a chilling impact on the few and scattered African Americans, who knew their safety depended upon white goodwill.[28]

In Fond du Lac, Wisconsin, for instance, local historian Sally Albertz believes "the KKK was instrumental in driving the blacks away." In the early 1920s the Klan held a "Klanvocation" at the Fond du Lac fairgrounds; newspapers claimed that 5,000 people marched in the parade. Subsequently, several crosses were burned in the areas where the blacks lived in the city. The earlier sense of possibility for African Americans in Fond du Lac—the welcome meal, the rooms at the hotel described in the previous chapter—had been replaced by a sense of terror.[29]

Sometimes this implicit threat became explicit. The Klan played a direct role in making some Oregon towns all-white in the 1920s. In Medford, Klansmen took George Burr, a bootblack, to the mountains, placed a noose around his neck, hung him from a branch, then cut him down and ordered him to leave town. He did. In Oregon City, six masked Klansmen confronted car wash owner Perry Ellis, the only black man in town, accused him of sleeping with a white woman, and nearly lynched him. Ellis moved to Tacoma, Washington, and Oregon City had no black household thereafter until the 1980s.[30]

Creating Sundown Towns by Ordinance

Under the thrall of the white supremacist rhetoric of the Nadir, many towns passed ordinances to prohibit African Americans from being within the corporate limits of the town after sundown or forbade selling or renting property to them. As with sundown towns themselves, actions against Chinese Americans led the way. Several authors tell of ordinances in the West banning them. Eureka, in northern California, passed its ordinance informally, at a large civic meeting on February 14, 1885, the day it expelled its large Chinese population, nicely showing the link between violence and ordinance, and did not repeal it until 1959.[31]

Reports of ordinances against African Americans began to surface after about 1900. I collected oral and written history from 25 towns in Illinois that have a tradition of such ordinances. In 1965, Donald Royer did a small study for the Indiana Civil Rights Commission, checking out nineteen Indiana towns with oral traditions of having passed sundown ordinances. He could not find any on paper. Between 2000 and 2004, I collected oral and written history from some of the same towns, finding the tradition still vibrant, and added another town. I also found evidence of sundown ordinances in 22 other towns in California, Arizona, Oklahoma, Kansas, Nebraska, Iowa, Missouri, Wisconsin, Tennessee, Ohio, and Maryland.[32] In California, for example, historian Olen Cole Jr. tells how the Civilian Conservation Corps in the 1930s tried to locate a company of African American workers in a large park that bordered Burbank and Glendale. Both cities refused; "the reason given was an 'old ordinance of the cities of Burbank and Glendale which prohibited Negroes from remaining inside municipal limits after sun down.' "[33]

Most of these towns, especially in the Midwest, were not close to any black population concentration and would not have confronted any inundation by African Americans had they failed to pass an ordinance. Consider De Land, for instance, a small village in central Illinois, population 475 in 2000. Present and former members of the De Land board of trustees agreed in 2002 that it had passed such an ordinance decades ago. De Land never had more than a few hundred inhabitants and is not located on any major railroad or highway, so it never faced an influx of nonwhites. Why, then, did it enact such a law? Since by the 1890s African Americans were defined in American culture as the problem, passing such an ordinance seemed prudent—the progressive thing to do. Towns that took similar actions were "up to date." De Land is in Piatt County, whose county seat, Monticello, was also a sundown town and also has a tradition of having enacted an ordinance. I suspect De Land followed Monticello's lead, and I believe that a wave of these ordinances swept the Midwest somewhere between 1900 and 1930. I have yet to find the text of a single midwestern ordinance, however,[34] so I cannot follow their spread via a written and dated record.[35]

Ordinances, Legal or Illegal?

It turns out that these ordinances were all illegal. Again, action against Chinese Americans in the West led the way, in this case in a positive direction. In 1890, Chinese Americans challenged in court a San Francisco ordinance that required them to move outside the city entirely or live in "an area set aside for slaughterhouses and other businesses thought prejudicial to public health or comfort," in the words of John Noonan, summarizing *In re Lee Sing*. The plaintiffs won; the ordinance was declared unconstitutional.[36]

In 1910, Baltimore passed a residential segregation ordinance. Quickly this was seen as the thing to do, and similar ordinances followed in Winston-Salem, Birmingham, Atlanta, Richmond, Norfolk, Louisville, New Orleans, St. Louis, Dallas, and other southern and border cities and towns. The Louisville ordinance became a test case. It designated city blocks with a majority of African Americans "black blocks" and those with a majority of whites "white blocks." Blacks were not allowed to move into white blocks and vice versa. These ordinances were drafted to look equal so they could pass muster under the Fourteenth Amendment, as historian T. J. Woofter Jr. explained:

> Although theoretically the law is supposed to apply to white and colored alike, in practice it never does. The colored people do not protest against white invasion, while the white people in mixed blocks do not hesitate to protest. Altogether about 50 cases have been made against Negroes under the New Orleans ordinance, and there has not been a single case against a white person.

In 1917, in *Buchanan v. Warley*, the U.S. Supreme Court held the Louisville ordinance unconstitutional. White civil rights lawyer Moorfield Story argued the case for the NAACP. In 1917, no plea for black rights would have been likely to prevail. Story won because a *white* right was at stake: the right of a white seller to sell his house to the highest bidder, even if that person happened to be black. The court held that the ordinance "destroyed the right of the individual to acquire, enjoy, and dispose of his property," in violation of the due process clause of the Fourteenth Amendment.[37] Although *Buchanan* ruled unconstitutional a law intended to create sundown neighborhoods, there can be no doubt that as a precedent, it would also invalidate ordinances intended to create sundown towns, which did not hide their explicit anti-black intentions behind even a gloss of fairness.[38]

In November 1915, Mayor J. R. Voigt introduced a segregation ordinance to the North Chattanooga City Council in Tennessee. Mayor Voigt was aware of the ongoing constitutional challenges to such a bill, similar ordinances having already been declared illegal in Winston, North Carolina, and Richmond, Virginia. He phrased the measure evenhandedly:

> Section 1: It shall be unlawful for any colored person to move into and occupy as a residence, place of abode, or to establish and maintain as a place of public assembly, any house upon any block upon which a greater number of houses are occupied as residences, places of abode, or places of public assembly by white people than are occupied as residences, places of abode or places of public assembly by colored people.

Section 2 then repeated this language but with the races reversed, so it appeared to be in line with the "separate but equal" ruling in *Plessy v. Ferguson* two decades earlier. However, everyone knew that North Chattanooga had only two black families living in it. Therefore it had no block "upon which a greater number of houses are occupied . . . by black people." As the *Chattanooga Daily Times* put it, "The passage of this ordinance will consequently make the town practically of an exclusively white population." In short, it was a sundown ordinance.

To avoid legal challenge, Mayor Voigt also built in provisions so that the two black families then living in North Chattanooga would not be forced to leave. They got the message anyway, for by the time the ordinance passed, on December 22, 1915, the *Daily Times* was able to headline its story, "North Chattanooga Is Exclusively White Now." The newspaper was proud to report, "As there are now no Negroes in North Chattanooga, it might be called the only town of its size in the country where the population is exclusively white." [39] "Mayor Voigt has received many compliments on his segregation ordinance," the story concluded. [40]

Despite *Buchanan v. Warley,* many cities and towns seem simply to have ignored the constitutional issue. Cities kept right on passing them, [41] and as the authors of the *Encyclopedia of Black America* noted in 1981, "A number of these ordinances were maintained long after 1917. . . . Legal attempts to enforce them in the courts were still being made in the 1950s." There is a scholarly tradition in American legal history that questions whether the U.S. Supreme Court can cause or has ever caused significant social change. The history of *Buchanan v. Warley* makes a good case for this theory. [42]

Brea, California, offers an example of an ordinance, known to be illegal, yet still in force decades after *Buchanan.* Vincent Jaster, retired school superintendent of Brea, was an educated man who knew sundown ordinances were unconstitutional. He also knew their power, as can be seen in his answer when asked in 1982, "Why would you prefer to live in Brea rather than Yorba Linda, Fullerton, or elsewhere?"

> Lower taxes, for one thing, better climate, nice people, and good schools. I maybe shouldn't say this, but this was an item some years ago in the 1940s and is not going to trouble me at all. Brea used to have a law that no black person could live in town here after six o'clock. See, Fullerton had its colored section; Placentia at that time was predominantly a Mexican town. But for years there were no black people in Brea at all. The shoeshine man was black, but he had to

leave town by six o'clock. It was an illegal law, of course, if you'd gone to the
Supreme Court.

No one took Brea to the Supreme Court, so its unconstitutional law was legal,
so far as its effect in Brea was concerned. The same point held in countless
other towns.[43]

Why shouldn't towns ignore the constitutional question? After all, during the Depression the federal government acted as if *Buchanan* did not exist
when it set up at least seven towns—Richland, Washington; Boulder City,
Nevada; Norris, Tennessee; Greendale, Wisconsin; Greenhills, Ohio;
Arthurdale, West Virginia; and Greenbelt, Maryland—that explicitly kept out
African Americans.[44] At the same time, and for three more decades, the Federal Housing Administration—a government agency—*required* restrictive
covenants before insuring housing loans. If the United States government,
charged with enforcing *Buchanan,* could exclude African Americans, obviously any community could.

Attempts to enforce illegal sundown ordinances in the streets were still
being made in the 1990s. In 2001, a central Illinoisan related that when she
and her husband were about to buy a house in Maroa a few years earlier, the
realtor "told us we wouldn't have any problems with black neighbors because
Maroa had an ordinance and they weren't allowed." Indeed, if a seller, agent,
and black would-be buyer in Maroa all believe today that the ordinance is
legal, in a very real sense it remains in effect, even though it *is* illegal. Residents
will think that selling to an African American violates the law; some will conclude that it is also wrong. They will not sell to a black and may take steps to
keep others from so doing. As an attorney who grew up in Martinsville, Illinois, a sundown town, put it, "If you say there's an ordinance, then whether
there was or not, that gives it the color of law." Even an unconstitutional ordinance connotes to the residents of the sundown town that the black would-be
newcomer is not *supposed* to be here—especially if those residents don't know
that the law is illegal. Whether legal or not, and even whether actually passed
or not, *belief in the ordinance puts it in force.* Indeed, residents in some midwestern towns think their sundown ordinances are *still* in effect.[45]

Creating Sundown Towns by Official Governmental Action

Even without enabling legislation, many municipal and county officials drove
out or kept out African Americans by formal policy. Discussing Crawford

County, Indiana, historian Emma Lou Thornbrough tells of "a contractor for the Louisville, New Albany, and St. Louis Railroad who had hired a gang of colored construction workers." White residents warned him that they would not be allowed to work. "When he sought protection from the county officials, they confirmed that it was an unwritten law that Negroes were not permitted in the county." A resident of Crawford County in the 1960s told a similar story about contractors building a different railroad in a later decade who also hired blacks: the sheriff warned African Americans about the law, but this time he allowed them to remain in the county, so long as they stayed on railroad property. Accordingly, they lived in tents near the work site. An "unwritten law" enforced by county officials including the sheriff *is* a law, to all intents and purposes.[46]

For that matter, an unwritten law enforced by a police chief or sheriff can be even more serious than a written law. Consider this conversation real estate developer Hank Roth had with the sheriff of Graham County in western North Carolina in about 1969: "He wanted me to know they didn't have any blacks in Robbinsville. He said the last 'nigger' who came to town 'hung under that tree over there.'" Thus no bright line can be drawn between unwritten understandings backed by official actions and formal ordinances.[47]

Towns that posted sundown signs implied they were all-white by municipal action. I have confirmed 184 towns in 32 states that displayed sundown signs.[48] Consider the Connecticut town whose sign is: "Whites Only Within City Limits After Dark (Portfolio 7)." To the passerby, that certainly *looks* official, and year after year, no one took it down, after all. Willie Harlen, president of the Washington County (Indiana) Historical Society, made this point when he wrote, "It is said there was a sundown sign east of Salem near Canton. Our Historical Society Treasurer was born in 1928. She remembers her parents telling about the sign . . . I don't know whether there was an ordinance posted or blacks were made to believe there was." Of course, whites too were made to believe there was. Towns that sounded whistles or sirens to warn blacks to get out of town at 6 PM also implied they were sundown by official action. Historian David Roediger grew up in Columbia, Illinois, a sundown town near St. Louis. Like Villa Grove, Columbia had a 6 PM whistle. Roediger reported that his mother moved to Columbia from Cairo in 1941 to teach elementary school. The police chief "almost immediately took her aside to say that she should feel secure, unlike in Cairo, because Columbia had a 6 PM whistle to warn blacks out of town." Coming from the chief of police, that is official policy.[49]

Jim Clayton, a retired *Washington Post* reporter who grew up in Johnston

City, a sundown town in southern Illinois, wrote, "Although there never was an anti-black ordinance, it was well understood that blacks were not permitted to stay in [Johnston City] over night." An ordinance would be superfluous, he suggested: everyone already knew no African Americans were allowed in town, so why bother saying so? If a black person tried to move into Johnston City in the 1940s, according to Clayton, "the Chief of Police would have told them to leave, and that would have been all it would take." The police chief also played a key role in Batesville, Indiana. According to Judy Tonges of the Batesville Historical Society,

> From what I can piece together, there was never an ordinance or law in Batesville prohibiting blacks. However, the knowledge was there. I talked with our police chief who grew up next to a lumber yard. He would visit the black truckers who were delivering lumber. He said they always rushed to get unloaded and out of town before dark.

Of course they did, after the police chief "visited" them.[50]

Like Johnston City's, many towns' sundown reputations were so well known that the municipalities felt no need to pass an ordinance. According to a longtime resident of Niles, Ohio, Niles qualifies: "I would be surprised if there were official ordinances prohibiting African-Americans from settling here. Things operate here much more informally. . . . Laws and ordinances are irrelevant and unnecessary." Many other sundown town residents made this point about their home communities, large and small. African Americans, or in some cases Jews or Chinese Americans, were not to live there, period. It was, and in some communities remains, as simple as that—written or not, legal or not. In many sundown towns and suburbs, law enforcement officials follow and stop African American motorists to this day as a matter of departmental policy. Thus we cannot assume that towns with ordinances were more racist, more rigid, or more notorious as sundown towns than communities whose officials kept out African Americans without such laws.[51]

Creating Sundown Towns by Freeze-out

Sometimes no specific act of violence or formal policy was required to turn a town or county all-white. As the Nadir deepened, white churches, schools, and even stores across the North often made African Americans unwelcome. In 1887 in Grundy County, Missouri, for example, a white school that previously had admitted black children now barred them. Their parents sued under the Fourteenth Amendment, but in 1890 the Missouri Supreme Court denied their appeal. Yet fifteen black children were required before a county had to have a "colored" high school. So African American children in Grundy County simply had no high school. It comes as no surprise that the black population of Grundy County fell from 254 in 1890 to just 85 by 1930, 35 in 1950, and 18 by 1960.[52]

Historian Robert Nesbit documented what happened to Pleasant Ridge, a small black community that grew up in Grant County, Wisconsin, after the Civil War. The neighboring white school agreed to take in their children, and in the years after the Civil War, Pleasant Ridge hosted an annual picnic that "featured an agreeable mixing of the neighbors." But by the late 1880s, its white neighbors had rechristened it "Nigger Ridge" and no longer deigned to attend community events such as the picnic. Residents continued the picnic for a few years, "as a mostly Negro affair" in Nesbit's words, but Pleasant Ridge "went into decline."[53] No specific event forced African Americans out, but Grant County's black population fell from 98 in 1870 to 68 in 1890, 43 in 1920, and just 7, all males, by 1960. To be black in Pleasant Ridge in 1870 when there were 97 other African Americans in the county was all right, because one also had white friends and neighbors. By 1920, being one of 43 African Americans meant living in a sea of Caucasians who ranged from indifferent to actively hostile.[54]

In some towns, whites who still wanted to befriend their black neighbors now felt compelled to do so surreptitiously, lest they too be ostracized by the larger white community. The one black student in the Wyandotte (Michigan) public schools in the 1910s had white school "friends" who were pleased that he did not embarrass them by recognizing that he knew them when their paths chanced to cross away from school. A woman in southern Illinois told me she played with the children of the black family that lived near them, but only under cover of darkness. Faced with such discouragements, especially in towns and counties where they were few, African Americans could no longer struggle on. So they pulled back into larger cities. At least there one's pariah status wasn't always right in front of one's face, and one might have friends.[55]

No bright-line boundary can be drawn between public prohibition and private freeze-out. A "Mass Meeting" in Bell City, Missouri, 110 miles south of St. Louis, on December 20, 1939, exemplifies this blurring. Citizens passed eight "Resolutions," all dealing with forcing out every African American from Bell City and northeastern Stoddard County and keeping any new blacks from moving in. The first "resolved that all land and property owners . . . be invited, urged, and requested not to permit or allow any Negro or Mexican families or single person or persons to move and reside upon their lands or property in the above described territory for any purpose whatsoever." Another warned "that the moral standard of living conditions will be greatly lowered if Negroes or Mexicans are allowed to inhabit this territory." Resolution 7 was the most ominous:

> That every Negro family or individual which numbers some six or eight now residing in said district be invited to move out of said territory in a reasonable length of time and that the landowners where said Negroes now dwell be invited to rid their premises of said Negro in a reasonable time.

The final resolution invoked officers of the law:

> Further resolved that all citizens and peace officers in this and adjoining counties are asked to cooperate with this convention and its committees in carrying out these resolutions in a peaceful and lawful manner.

Clearly "John Wright, Ben Oakley, Rev. Jones, and Committee," who affixed their names to the resolutions and had flyers printed up—official-looking, suitable for posting—thought they would have the law on their side. Apparently they did, for by 2000, Bell City still had only 5 African Americans among its 461 residents. Yet just to the southeast lies one of Missouri's blackest areas.[56]

Communities that froze out their African Americans might seem at first glance to be "kinder" than those that forced them out violently or as a matter of law. But as Wyandotte historian Edwina DeWindt points out, for such a crusade to succeed requires "a general unity of action of all Wyandotte citizens in not renting or selling property to Negroes, refusing to serve them in stores and restaurants, and not hiring Negroes in places of employment." Such unanimity over time might require more widespread anti-black feeling—which Wyandotte had in abundance—and more systematic discrimination than is manifested in a town where a mob suddenly erupts to force out African Americans overnight. Moreover, some campaigns to force African Americans out by firing them were mounted in the 1920s by the KKK or labor unions that also threatened violence, so the intimidation level may have been no lower than in Fond du Lac. Whites who wanted to retain their black employees often found themselves violently intimidated and forced to let them go—so freezing out proves no kinder on close inspection.[57]

Creating Sundown Towns and Suburbs by Buyout

Some independent sundown towns bought out their African Americans to achieve all-white status. Especially in suburbia, buyouts were also often used to get rid of black would-be residents. I have collected examples of buyouts to keep blacks from completing purchases in Somerset, New Jersey; Astoria, Oregon; and many points in between. Indeed, buying out the lone African American family that dared to buy in a sundown suburb was so common that Lorraine Hansberry made such an offer the central plot element in her play *A Raisin in the Sun*.[58]

Buying out was not always kinder and gentler, because usually the offer was not to be refused, accompanied by a clear threat. In 1922, residents of Liberty Township in northern Indiana "have been worked up to a frenzy regarding the removal of a colored family, consisting of six persons into that vicinity," as reported in the *Chesterton Tribune*. "The race problem, as far as Liberty township is concerned," was "amicably settled" when the black would-be resident sold the property to a trustee of the township and returned to Gary "with his wife and four children." Now "Liberty township is at peace with the world again," the newspaper concluded. "Amicably settled" may be a euphemism for the resale process, however, given that all of Porter County was sundown at the time and for five decades thereafter. Perhaps the "frenzy" played some role in inducing the black family to sell.

Often, as in Porter County, the offer came from the local government. In that case, the black family usually had no choice; if they refused to sell, the jurisdiction then claimed that the land was required for a park or other public purpose, condemned it, and bought it.

Chapter 7 tells how Sheridan, Arkansas, induced its black population to leave in 1954 in response to *Brown v. Board of Education*. One man, Jack Williams, owner of the local sawmill and the sawmill workers' homes, was principally responsible. He made his African American employees an extraordinary buyout offer: he would *give* them their homes and move them to Malvern, 25 miles west, at no cost to them. This turned out to be a proposition they couldn't refuse, according to my source, who lived in Sheridan at the time, for if a family refused to move, he would evict them and burn down their home. Another longtime resident corroborated this account: "He wouldn't have them in school here. He had little shacks for them. He told them they could have the shacks and move them out, or he would burn them down." Not unreasonably, blacks "chose" to accept the buyout and move to Malvern in response to this ultimatum. A few other African Americans lived in Sheridan—

not in Williams's employ—but what could they do? The preacher, the beautician, and the cafe owner suddenly found themselves without a clientele. They left too.

Creating Sundown Suburbs

Suburbs used the largest array of different weapons for becoming and staying all-white, beginning around 1900, although ultimately they too relied on violence. It is important to understand that the whiteness of America's suburbs was no accident. On the contrary, all-white suburbs were *achieved*. As Dorothy Newman wrote in 1978, "Residential separation rests on a system of formal rules (though no longer worded in racial terms—the words are illegal) and informal but carefully adhered-to practices which no amount of legislation has been able yet to penetrate."

Moreover, the suburbs weren't always so white. Between 1870 and 1900, African Americans lived more widely scattered across metropolitan areas than they did by 1930 or later, just as African Americans lived more scattered across northern states in 1890 than they did by 1930 or later. When suburbanization set in, African American families already resided on the fringes of many cities. In many places—across the South, of course, but even as far north as Dearborn, Michigan, and Edina, Minnesota—developers had to get rid of African Americans, who already lived where the suburbs were being formed, to create the white suburbs we now take for granted. In 1870, before Dearborn township incorporated, among its 2,300 people lived 30 black residents, but by 1920, incorporated Dearborn's 2,470 residents included just one African American.[59]

When they sought to establish the town of Edina, for example—now the richest suburb of Minneapolis–St. Paul—developers faced the problem that a Quaker village already existed in Richfield Township where the new suburb was to be built. Throughout the North, Quakers had welcomed African Americans after the Civil War. Many black families now lived in the western half of Richfield Township. "Over the ensuing decades," according to Deborah Morse-Kahn, whose history of Edina is exceptional for its willingness to discuss the community's racial past, African Americans "became very involved in community life—very often as leaders." Indeed, "Edina Mills was a fully integrated and color-blind community well before the turn of the century." Whites attended black weddings. An African American woman founded the first PTA in Edina in the late 1880s and served as its first vice president. B. C. Yancey was a justice of the peace and village recorder.[60]

Then, just after World War I, Samuel Thorpe developed "the elegant Edina Country Club residential district," as Morse-Kahn correctly describes it, "with restrictive deed covenants in place." Now Edina's African American community "would feel estranged. Thorpe Brothers' building restrictions guaranteed to any buyer, in an era when municipal zoning was nonexistent, that their property would be 'safe' from devaluating circumstances, stating that blacks were explicitly ineligible to buy in the district." According to Joyce Repya, associate planner for Edina, deeds carried various restrictions such as "No fuel storage tanks above ground," "No shedding poplars, box elders, or other objectionable trees," and, most important, the racial exclusionary clause quoted at the head of the next chapter. And unlike all other restrictions, which phased out in 1964, the restriction to "the white or Caucasian race" continued in force forever. "By the late 1930s," in Morse-Kahn's words, "virtually all of Edina's black families had moved into Minneapolis and an historic era had ended for the village." At that point, Morse-Kahn goes on, anti-Semitism, which had been "virtually unheard-of in Edina before the First World War, became a haunting hallmark of Edina life. As late as the end of the 1950s, potential buyers known to be Jewish were often openly turned away by realtors and requested to look for residential property elsewhere."[61]

Other suburbs across America had to force out already existing pockets of African American residents to achieve all-white status. Especially across the South, African Americans have long lived in rural areas. For all-white suburbs to be built, those residents must be cleared out. And although the traditional South had few independent sundown towns, after the 1930s it developed its share of sundown suburbs. By that time some white Southerners were beginning to abandon their traditional view of African Americans as subjects for exploitation in favor of the northern view of them as nuisances to be rid of. And of course, African Americans were not as essential to the southern suburban economy as they had been to its plantation economy.

Chamblee, Georgia, began as a small town outside Atlanta. In 1940, Chamblee had 1,081 residents including 222 African Americans. After World War II, Chamblee became a suburb of Atlanta. By 1950, its population soared to 3,445, while its black population shrank to 92. Ten years later, Chamblee had 6,635 people, including just 2 African Americans. And by 1970, it had 9,127, including just 1 black woman, probably a maid. Developers built brand-new all-white subdivisions in the 1950s, according to a woman who grew up in two of them. I could not locate anyone in Chamblee who knew why its African Americans departed. Schooling provides one possible reason. Until massive school desegregation, which took place around

1970, African American families in suburbs throughout the South found living there hugely inconvenient. Most suburbs with small black populations had no black schools; instead they paid tuition for their black children to attend black schools in the inner city. This policy motivated many African American families to move to that city rather than impose long commutes on their children, often with no school buses. African Americans in Chamblee had no school, according to a former mayor, and had to attend the nearest black school in Atlanta. After 1970, Chamblee desegregated all over again, a story we will pick up in a later chapter, but in the 1940s and '50s, it seems to have embodied a "push-out" or "buyout" of its black population.[62]

The same thing happened outside Washington, D.C.; Gainesville, Florida; Memphis; New York City; and other expanding metropolises. Although southern white developers showed no more hesitation than northerners about removing black residents for new sundown suburbs, they usually respected black burial grounds. The result, found as far north as Maryland, is an occasional black church and cemetery standing isolated in an otherwise all-white suburb. Sometimes African Americans then abandoned their church and cemetery because they could not cope with repeated vandalism by white suburban teenagers.

Across the nation, according to a 1981 government report, "although white migration flows favored the suburbs throughout, until the late 1960s more blacks were moving to the city from the much smaller suburban base than were suburbanizing in the majority of the [metropolitan areas]." In other words, until about 1968, African Americans were getting displaced *from* still-whitening suburbs at a faster rate than they were moving *to* suburbia.[63]

Even maids and servants came to be seen as an unwanted presence after dark if they lived in independent households. In 1910, a committee of residents of Wilmette, an elite North Shore suburb of Chicago, asked all families unable to house their maids and gardeners on their own premises to fire them, especially if they lived in Wilmette, claiming that their presence had "depressed real estate values" in the village. According to Chicago historian Thomas Philpott, it worked: "Few blacks who did not have quarters in their white employers' homes remained in Wilmette." Even by 1970, Wilmette's 32,134 residents included just 81 African Americans, and most of them were live-in maids.[64]

All Planned Suburbs Were Intentionally Created All-White

Elite suburbs that were built by a single developer were especially likely to begin life as all-white on purpose. Tuxedo Park, New York, perhaps the richest of them all, may have gone sundown first, even before 1890. Affluent whites founded it "as a club community and maintained that discipline for nearly 50 years," as Albert Winslow put it in the town's official history, published in 1992. "Anybody seeking to buy property in the Park would by necessity be required to be a member of the Club. The association also maintained a police department and six gate houses." The gate houses were connected by barbed wire, according to historian Patrick McMullen, who credits Tuxedo Park with thus inventing the gated community in 1881. "Tuxedo Park also heralded the creation of a new entity, the homeowner's association, meant to influence the appearance, population, and social character of the community."

Just in case anyone tried to move in without being a member, Tuxedo Park developed additional methods for keeping out undesirables, primarily Jews and African Americans but also others who "did not enjoy the attributes for membership in the Club," as Winslow put it. He goes on to tell of a wealthy buyer who purchased a large house in Tuxedo Park in the late 1920s and tried to move in. "He was told his membership in the Club was out of the question. He persevered and then had to be told that if he did indeed buy he would be denied access to water and sewer lines, which were owned by the Tuxedo Park Association. . . . He did not buy!"[65]

As the twentieth century wore on, Americans continued to build planned communities. Every planned town that I know of—indeed, *every community in America founded after 1890 and before 1960 by a single developer or owner—kept out African Americans from its beginnings.* Chronologically, these include Highland Park near Dallas in 1907–13 and Mariemont near Cincinnati in 1914, both of which won fame for their innovative shopping centers. Shaker Heights, east of Cleveland, was designed to be "utopian" and excluded blacks, Jews, and Catholics from its inception. Near Los Angeles, planned all-white suburbs set up around this time include Beverly Hills, Culver City, Palos Verdes Estates, Tarzana (developed by Edgar Rice Burroughs from the proceeds of his *Tarzan* novels), and several others. Ebenezer Howard's "garden city" concept, imported from England, influenced at least seven suburbs or exurbs built around World War II: Radburn, New Jersey, in 1929; Greenbelt, Maryland, near Washington, D.C., Greenhills, Ohio, near Cincinnati, Greendale, Wisconsin, near Milwaukee, and Norris, Tennessee, in the 1930s; Richland, Washington, in 1942; and Park Forest, near Chicago, in the 1950s. All of these planned communities were developed as sundown towns.[66] The Franklin Roosevelt administration built the "Greens"—Greenbelt, Greenhills, and Greendale—to create jobs and supply needed housing during the Great Depression; all three remained all-white for decades. So did Norris, built by the Tennessee Valley Authority to house workers on nearby Norris Dam, Richland, put up to house workers at the Hanford atomic plant, and Boulder City, Nevada, built for workers on Boulder Dam.[67]

Most "Unplanned" Suburbs Were Also Created All-White

When a suburb expanded without a plan or single developer, African Americans had more opportunity to move in. Still, the overwhelming majority of unplanned suburbs were created all-white from their inception. Most kept out African Americans (and often Jews) openly and "legally," as Portfolio 28, an ad for a suburban development in Salt Lake City, exemplifies. Their most straightforward method was to pass a formal ordinance, like some of their country cousins, the independent sundown towns. Many suburbs never passed a formal ordinance but, like Batesville, Indiana, or Johnston City, Illinois, acted as if they had.

Most suburbs incorporated between 1900 and 1968. Often they formed in the first place to become sundown towns. According to John Denton, who studied housing in the San Francisco Bay area, "One of the principal purposes (if not the entire purpose) of suburban incorporations is to give their populations control of the racial composition of their communities." When they incorporated, suburbs typically drew their boundaries to exclude African American neighborhoods. In 1912, white voters in Brentwood, Maryland, rejected incorporation with tiny adjoining North Brentwood, majority black, so in 1924, North Brentwood incorporated separately. Two Texas sundown suburbs—Highland Park and University Park—are entirely surrounded by Dallas, which tried to annex them repeatedly between 1919 and 1945. The "Park Cities," as they call themselves, repeatedly rebuffed Dallas. Under Texas law, if one municipality entirely surrounds another, the larger can absorb the smaller. Although Dallas encircles the Park Cities, it can annex neither, because on one side each borders "another" city—the other Park City. I put quotation marks around "another" because the Park Cities are alike and even form one school system.[68]

In 1960, white city officials of Phoenix, Illinois, another south suburb of Chicago, pulled off what suburban expert Larry McClellan calls "a stunning example of racial politics." Instead of using municipal boundaries to keep African Americans out, they redrew the city limits to create white flight without ever moving! In the 1950s, Phoenix was going black, so in 1960, its white city officials "de-annexed" the part of the city where most whites lived, ceding themselves to Harvey, the next suburb west, and leaving Phoenix to the African Americans. It didn't work: Harvey also proceeded to go majority-black.[69]

Regardless of the Creation, the Result Was the Same

How a town went sundown—owing to a violent expulsion, a quiet ordinance, or a more subtle freeze-out or buyout—made no consistent difference over time. Either way, African Americans lost their homes and jobs, or their chance for homes and jobs. Either way, the town defined itself as sundown for many decades, and that decision had to be defended.

The white townspeople of Sheridan, Arkansas, for instance, were probably no more racist than residents of many other Arkansas towns until 1954. Indeed, they may have been *less* racist than many: as Chapter 7 tells, they almost chose to desegregate their schools in response to *Brown,* a step taken by only two towns in Arkansas. After the 1954 buyout, however, Sheridan's notoriety grew. As a lifelong resident said in 2001, the town "developed a reputation that was perhaps more aggressive than it really deserved. For years, black people wouldn't even stop in Sheridan for gas." In fact, Sheridan probably deserved its new reputation. Although originally prompted by a single individual, no Sheridan resident lifted a voice to protest the forced buyout of its black community. On the contrary, two different Sheridan residents said in separate conversations in 2001, "You know, that solved the problem!" Implicitly they defined "the problem" as school desegregation, or more accurately, the existence of African American children. With a definition like that, inducing blacks to leave indeed "solved the problem." Having accepted that "solution," whites in Sheridan were left predisposed to further racism. According to reports, they posted signs, "Nigger, Don't Let the Sun Set On You Here." Long after non-sundown towns in Arkansas desegregated their schools, Sheridan fans developed a reputation for bigotry when their high school played interracial teams in athletic contests. This reputation grew in the late 1980s and early 1990s, when Sheridan played rival Searcy, a majority-white town, but not a sundown town. Searcy had a talented African American on its roster, and when he got the ball in games played in Sheridan, white parents and Sheridan students would yell "Get the nigger" and similar phrases.[70]

The methods blur into each other on a continuum. Towns that went all-white nonviolently frequently employed violence to stay that way. A city official in tiny De Land remembers as a child in about 1960 overhearing an adult conversation to the effect that a black family recently moved into De Land, but there was a mysterious fire in their house and they left. "De Land had a sundown rule," the adults went on, "so what did they expect?" In this case, the passage of an ordinance probably contributed to private violence by heightening white outrage at the violation of community mores. Whether a given town became all-white violently or nonviolently, formally or informally, does not predict how it will behave later.[71]

Because suburbs got organized later than most independent towns, after the Nadir was well under way, a much higher proportion of them were created as sundown towns from the beginning, as the next chapter shows.

5

Sundown Suburbs

No lot shall ever be sold, conveyed, leased, or rented to any person other than one of the white or Caucasian race, nor shall any lot ever be used or occupied by any person other than one of the white or Caucasian race, except such as may be serving as domestics for the owner or tenant of said lot, while said owner or tenant is residing thereon. All restrictions, except those in paragraph 8 (racial exclusion), shall terminate on January 1, 1964.

—Typical restrictive covenant for property in Edina, Minnesota, sundown suburb of Minneapolis[1]

ACROSS AMERICA, most suburbs, and in some metropolitan areas almost all of them, excluded African Americans (and often Jews). This pattern of suburban exclusion became so thorough, even in the traditional South, and especially in the older metropolitan areas of the Northeast and Midwest, that Americans today express no surprise when inner cities are mostly black while suburbs are overwhelmingly white.

After 1900, precisely as the suburbs unfolded, African Americans were moving to northern metropolitan areas as part of the Great Retreat and, beginning around 1915, as part of the Great Migration. But the suburbs kept them out. Detroit, for example, slowly became overwhelmingly black, even though it touches at least four sundown suburbs—Dearborn, Grosse Pointe, Melvindale, and Warren. Map 4 shows these contiguous sundown suburbs and many others. Some black families from Detroit would have moved to these suburbs the way whites did, had they been allowed. Indeed, Inkster, a majority-black suburb founded in 1921, lies just beyond Dearborn, farther from Detroit. Yet while Inkster to the west and Detroit to the north and east grew in black population, Dearborn, between them, grew even whiter. Many of its residents took pride in the saying, "The sun never set on a Negro in Dearborn," according to historians August Meier and Elliott Rudwick. Dear-

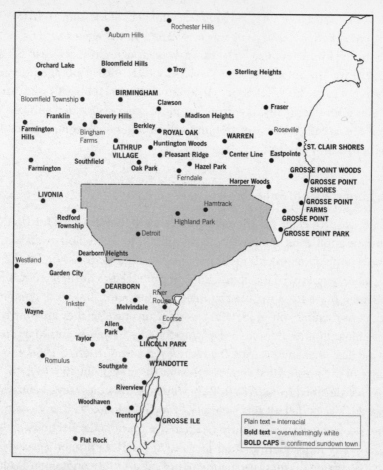

Map 4. Detroit Suburbs

At least 47 of 59 suburbs outside Detroit were overwhelmingly white, decade after decade. Eleven were interracial and one requires more census study. I have confirmed only 15 of the 47 as sundown suburbs, but further research would surely confirm most of the rest. In 1960, for example, Garden City, which abuts interracial Inkster, had just two African Americans, both women, probably both live-in maids, among its nearly 40,000 residents. Twenty years later, large suburbs like Berkley, Clawson, Farmington, and Harper Woods had not one black inhabitant. Such numbers imply exclusion.

Moreover, of the 11 interracial suburbs, several were not meaningfully integrated; the black/white border merely happened to run through the suburb. In 1940, for example, 1,800 African Americans lived in Ecorse, but not one east of the tracks, where the whites lived. In 1970, whites in River Rouge could recall only one black family, "the first in 50 years," that lived on the east side, and they were intimidated into leaving.*

* Andrew Wiese, *Places of Their Own* (Chicago: University of Chicago Press, 2004), 49.

born's longtime mayor Orville Hubbard, who held office from 1942 to 1978, told a reporter that "as far as he was concerned, it was against the law for Negroes to live in his suburb." Dearborn was an extraordinary case because Hubbard was so outspoken, but David Good, Hubbard's biographer, cautions us not to see him as unique: "In a sense, Orville Hubbard's view was no different from that in any of a dozen or more other segregated suburbs that ringed the city of Detroit—or in hundreds of other such communities scattered across the country."[2]

The Importance of Suburbs

In time, suburbs came to dominate our nation. Between 1950 and 1970, the suburban population doubled from 36 million to 74 million as 83% of the nation's population growth took place in the suburbs. By 1970, for the first time, more people lived in suburbs than in central cities or rural areas. Thirty years later, more lived in suburbs than in cities and rural areas combined. Since suburbanites vote at higher rates than anyone else, they are now by far the dominant political force in the United States. Thomas and Mary Edsall provide these statistics: during the twenty years from 1968 to 1988, the percentage of the presidential vote cast in suburbs grew from 36% to 48%. The rural vote declined from 35% to 22% while central cities stayed constant at about 29.5%. "What all this suggests," they conclude, "is that a politics of suburban hegemony will come to characterize presidential elections."[4]

Not only in politics do suburbs rule. In his 1995 primer *The Suburbs,* John Palen notes the increasing influence of suburbs in economic and cultural spheres:

> Suburbs have gone from being fringe commuter areas to being the modal locations for American living and working. There has been a suburban revolution that has changed suburbs from being places on the periphery of the urban cores to being the economic and commercial centers of a new metropolitan area form. Increasingly, it is the suburbs that are central with the cities being peripheral.

As early as 1978, a *New York Times* survey of suburban New Yorkers found that more than half did not feel they belonged to the New York metropolitan area at all, and a fourth never went to the city even once in the previous year. By 1987, suburban shopping malls accounted for 54% of all sales of personal and household items. Suburbs now contain two-thirds of our office space. Palen notes that "more than ¾ of the job growth during the 1980s in

America's twenty largest metropolitan areas occurred in the suburbs." He claims that the suburbs are also becoming dominant culturally. Many of the sporting and cultural events that used to take place downtown now play in suburban arenas and concert halls. In short, "although it somewhat twists the language, suburbs are more and more frequently the center of the metropolitan area."[5]

The Good Life

Why did this happen? The American rush to the suburbs wasn't just to avoid African Americans. Indeed, it wasn't *primarily* to avoid African Americans. It took place in metropolitan areas with few African Americans as well as areas such as Detroit whose core cities became majority-black. Families moved to the suburbs for two principal reasons: first, it seemed the proper way to bring up children, and second, it both showed and secured social status. That is, Americans saw suburbs as the solution to two problems: having a family and having prestige. Suburban dwellers wanted to raise their children to be safe, happy, and well educated in metropolitan areas. They also wanted to be upwardly mobile and to display their upward mobility.

The two functions were closely related, since "living well" begets status. As the twentieth century wore on, Americans told themselves increasingly that children need their own grass to play on and their own trees to play under, and families need their own plots of earth in which to put down roots. Today this idea is so firmly embedded in our national culture, at least that of our lower-upper and middle classes, as to seem "natural."[6] Of course, by "natural" we really mean so deep in our culture that we do not—perhaps cannot—question it. And of course, communities that embody such "obvious" values are by definition better—hence more prestigious—places to live.

Not all suburbs fit the same mold, of course. Some are centered around industry, such as Dearborn, Michigan, around Ford, and Granite City, Illinois, around the graniteware plant and several steel mills. Some of these working-class suburbs were founded as white enclaves; some, like Dearborn and Granite City, became sundown suburbs by forcing out their African Americans; still others remained interracial, especially if they had begun as interracial independent cities, as did Pontiac, Michigan. Among the benefits that sundown suburbs confer is participation in what political scientist Larry Peterson calls a "type of Americanization"—leaving the old Polish, Greek, or Italian city neighborhood for a new, ethnically mixed, but all-white neighborhood in the suburbs.[7]

Suburbs also offer other very real amenities. People move to them to get good schools, nice parks, good city services, and safety, as well as status and aesthetics. Children in elite suburbs have a leg up, because these communities concentrate opportunity. An elite suburban child is far more likely to know what the world has to offer and how to take advantage of it—from computers to summer jobs to coaching classes for the SAT. As a former school administrator in Stamford, Connecticut, said, "the keys to the kingdom" lie in these suburbs. And those keys are in addition to suburban tax base advantages that make possible much better public schools.

Avoiding the Problems of the City

"The city is doomed," announced Henry Ford. "We shall solve the city problem by leaving the city." And he moved Ford's headquarters and largest manufacturing unit to the sundown suburb of Dearborn. Suburbs took steps to define themselves as different from cities. The promoters of Highland Park, Texas, used the slogan "Beyond the City's Dust and Smoke" to distance their suburb from Dallas, even though Dallas eventually encompassed Highland Park. Upper-middle-class Americans were revolted by the dirt of the cities, not only from their factories and railroads, but also from their politics. If their political machines could not be reformed, then the "progressive" thing to do would be to form one's own government in the suburbs under the control of the "better element." In 1874, Brookline, Massachusetts, voted to reject union with Boston. By 1920, suburbs had rejected mergers with central cities across the United States, from Rochester to Pittsburgh to Chicago to Oakland.[8]

This withdrawal from the city is evident in suburban names. Earlier suburbs of Chicago were named, inter alia, North Chicago, East Chicago, South Chicago, and, yes, West Chicago. Later suburbs used *park* and *forest* to death. Chicago alone is surrounded by Bedford Park, Calumet Park, Deer Park, Edison Park, Elmwood Park, Evergreen Park, Forest Lake, Forest View, Franklin Park, Hanover Park, Highland Park, Ingalls Park, Jefferson Park, LaGrange Park, Lake Forest, Liberty Park, Melrose Park, Merrionette Park, Norwood Park, Oak Forest, Oak Park, Orland Park, Palos Park, Park City, Park Ridge, Richton Park, River Forest, Round Lake Park, Schiller Park, Stone Park, University Park, and Villa Park, not to mention Forest Park and Park Forest. The process continues: in 1973, East Paterson, New Jersey, changed its name to Elmwood Park. East Detroit became Erin Heights in 1984; eight years later, it changed to Eastpointe, trying desperately to grasp some of the prestige of

Grosse Pointe, Grosse Pointe Woods, Grosse Pointe Farms, and Grosse Pointe Park, sundown suburbs to its south.[9]

Moving to the suburbs to escape the disamenities of the city—everything from industrial sectors and delivery trucks to crime and prostitution—not only makes aesthetic sense and provides a more pleasant lifestyle; it also makes for a better investment. A real estate agent put it this way, advising potential home buyers in 2001 in the *Chicago Tribune*:

> You should nearly always avoid buying in a "marginal neighborhood," such as one that is seriously flawed by commercial blight, heavy traffic congestion, loud environmental noise, pollution, or foul smells.
>
> "I would only do it if I'd been renting for years and years and absolutely could not afford to buy anywhere else," he says.

His advice makes sense and does not mention race, but like everything said about suburbs thus far, it has racial implications. Marginal people make for a marginal neighborhood, and no people have been more marginalized than African Americans.[10]

Blacks as a Key Problem to Be Avoided

African Americans' low prestige has long posed a danger to white status. Andrew Hacker, author of *Two Nations,* identified the status threat in 1961:

> If there is one sword which hangs over the heads of untold millions of white— and Northern—Americans it is that they cannot afford to live in close proximity to Negroes. The single social fact which can destroy the whole image of middle class respectability is to be known to reside in a neighborhood which has Negroes nearby.

In the early 1970s, among many items inquiring about relationships with African Americans, " 'Having a Negro family as next door neighbors' was one of the most objected to," reported social psychologist Thomas Pettigrew. Writing in 2000, historian Stephen Meyer pointed out that race still plays the key role: "Many whites remain reluctant to accept African Americans as social equals. They refuse to accept African Americans as neighbors."[11]

In addition to their status concerns, white suburbanites also worry that African Americans are less intelligent, more prone to crime, and a threat to property values. That last concern—property values—rephrases the status issue as a very real pocketbook problem: whites feel an African American next door may make their own home less desirable when they go to sell it. The solution to this familiar blacks-as-problem thinking proves the same in the suburbs as in independent towns: keep them out.

Suburbs Start to Go Sundown

Most of America's first suburbs, built along railroad and streetcar lines, were not all white. Even elegant suburbs—"places like Greenwich, Connecticut; Englewood, New Jersey; Evanston, Illinois; and Chestnut Hill, Massachusetts," in urban historian Kenneth Jackson's words—made room for servants and workers, including independent African American households (in addition to those who lived in).[12] "The barons of Chestnut Hill regarded the close proximity of a poor servant class as an advantage." To commute all the way from the inner city was too expensive, and it was too hard to arrive in time to warm the house and fix breakfast. Some of these early suburbs grew up around stops on the new suburban rail lines. They replicated "the class-related spatial patterns of the core cities," writes Jackson, "with the poorest inhabitants living closest to the tiny business districts and the more affluent residents living in commodious homes on landscaped grounds." Thus Stamford, Connecticut, outside New York City, has its poorer section near what is now the Amtrak station, and Lower Merion, outside Philadelphia, includes Ardmore, near the SEPTA station, where its maids, chauffeurs, and gardeners lived.[13]

Gradually, such a hierarchy no longer seemed good enough. A black family living in Stamford or Evanston might become wealthy, after all, and might want to move into a more elite neighborhood. Already their children were in the public schools with the children of the elite, at least by high school. Affluent whites now declared their upward mobility by moving outward geographically, to all-white suburbs. They expressed their social distance from nonwhites and working-class whites by increasing the physical distance between them. Geographically and chronologically, Kenilworth was the next suburb north of Evanston. Chapter 8 notes that Joseph Sears, developer of Kenilworth, incorporated the restriction "Sales to *Caucasians only*" into his village's founding documents, according to Kenilworth's official historian. We have seen that independent sundown towns often allowed African Americans as live-in servants. Sears had forgotten to make this concession. Therefore, according to his daughter Dorothy: "When in 1903 he would have our colored coachman and his family move into the remodeled farmhouse, he sent a note to each resident, and none objected." Of course they didn't, for the coachman's family was hardly an independent household; moreover, Sears still controlled Kenilworth. Soon Kenilworth became the most elite suburb of Chicago.[14]

This was a national pattern. Like Kenilworth, Darien, the next suburb beyond Stamford, Connecticut, kept out African Americans. So did Palos Verdes Estates, outside of Los Angeles. Increasingly as the twentieth century wore on, white breadwinners chose to make burdensome commutes from ever more distant sundown suburbs. Elite sundown suburbs such as Kenilworth, Darien, and Palos Verdes Estates also differed from older suburbs in being exclusive by social class. The suburbanization of America and the segregation of our metropolitan areas went hand in hand, and the automobile—the same technological innovation that made mass suburbanization possible—facilitated this new separation by race and class. Today elite suburbs no longer need to include working-class homes. Even their teachers and police officers commute from housing they can afford, often two suburbs away. We have seen that some independent sundown towns had black communities nearby to supply workers, like the townships outside Johannesburg, South Africa. So do some sundown suburbs, in a way: "maid buses," sometimes subsidized by residents of the town, bring domestic workers from the nearest inner city every morning and return them home before sundown.

On the ground in Chevy Chase, Maryland, stands a tangible symbol of this difference between old and newer suburbs: the Saks Fifth Avenue store, looking like a bank surrounded by the green lawns of well-kept suburbia. In 1903, Francis Newlands, who set up the Chevy Chase Land Company to build an elite suburb just northwest of Washington, D.C., sold some land to developers to build a subdivision called Belmont to provide affordable housing for domestics and other workers. Shortly thereafter, according to *Washington Post* reporter Marc Fisher, "rumors swept the area that Belmont was to be a community for the suburb's black servants." Newlands claimed he had no such intent, and in 1909 his company filed suit, claiming that the developer was committing fraud "by offering to sell lots . . . to Negroes."[15] In the end, the Chevy Chase Company reacquired the land, and Chevy Chase became one of our first sundown suburbs. The Belmont property then lay vacant for decades, perhaps tainted by its past. That's why it was available for the Saks Fifth Avenue store and parking lot. Today Chevy Chase remains an enclave for rich whites. In 2000, its 6,183 residents included just 18 people[16] living in families with at least one African American householder.[17]

Nearby on the landscape is a reminder that throughout the decades when suburban America was being constructed—and constructed *white*—the federal government abetted the process. Newlands got the United States to create Rock Creek Park as our third national park and the largest urban park in the National Park System. At once the park increased the value of the land Newlands and his associates had bought by removing 2,000 acres from the market, created a beautiful amenity adjoining Chevy Chase, and interposed a green swath of forest to define the new suburb as "rural." Most important, Rock Creek Park buffered Chevy Chase from the increasingly black neighborhoods on what Chevy Chase residents came to call "the wrong side of the park." It still plays this role today.[18]

Sundown Cemeteries

Cemeteries had gone suburban even before the Nadir. According to the cemetery's web site, the founders of Mount Auburn Cemetery outside Boston, established in 1831, "believed that burying and commemorating the dead was best done in a tranquil and beautiful natural setting set apart from urban life." Mount Auburn's park-like imitators around the country actually helped inspire the suburban movement. If the suburbs embodied the good life, avoiding "the problems of the city," then the new cemeteries, complete with lakes, hills, and trees, represented the good death. Quiet and exclusive, they were very different from the burying grounds adjoining urban churches, where one might rub elbows in death with persons very different in race and social class. And during the Nadir, like their suburban environs, the new cemeteries too went sundown, leaving a vivid record of the process on the landscape in granite.[19]

In New Jersey in 1884, a cemetery refused burial to an African American sexton, which led to indignant criticism from the governor as well as the *New York Times*. The Nadir had not yet set in. By World War I, segregation was common practice in cemeteries and no longer aroused any protest, save from African Americans. In 1907, for example, the Forest Home Cemetery near Chicago adopted a resolution that only the remains of white persons would be buried in that cemetery from then on, "except that in cases where colored persons already owned lots in the cemetery, the remains of such colored persons and their direct heirs could be interred there."[20] Before this change, John Gaskill, African American, had buried four of his children in his lot in that cemetery. When his wife died, in 1912, he tried to bury her near them but was refused, because she was not his heir. He filed suit and took his case to the Illinois Supreme Court, which found against him, so his wife could not be buried near her children, or, if he followed through with his plans, near her husband. By 1930, most cemeteries had exclusionary clauses.[21]

Cemetery exclusion was not challenged in the courts until well after World War II. White Chapel Memory Gardens, a sundown cemetery in Syracuse, New York, did not allow a black body within its gates until 1981. Some cemeteries still maintain sundown policies.[22]

Keeping Out Jews

When Joseph Sears proclaimed Kenilworth open to *"Caucasians only,"* the phrase also meant no Jews. Lena and Modie Spiegel, of Spiegel Catalog fame, soon broke this barrier when they "rented Lawyer Merritt Star's large house at 40 Melrose for eight years," according to Colleen Kilner, Kenilworth historian. "How could there be objection when they purchased," she added, "especially after having proved themselves?" Kilner went on to note that their son was president of his eighth-grade class in 1925, but historian Michael Ebner says she painted far too rosy a portrait:

> In the years before World War I, Lena and Modie remained outsiders. Nor did their circumstances improve as perhaps they hoped they would, when the Spiegels became ardent practitioners of Christian Science in an effort to diminish their Jewish identity.

Kenilworth residents subsequently closed ranks against other Jews, according to Ebner: "It is generally thought that one outcome [of the Spiegels] was to buttress the practice of enforcing restrictive covenants," covenants that read "white Protestants only." Labor historian Harry Rubenstein says Kenilworth and nearby Lake Forest started letting Italians in after World War II. Not Jews, though: in 1959, the Anti-Defamation League reported, "The North Shore suburbs of Kenilworth, Lake Forest, Barrington, and Palatine are almost completely closed to Jews. Kenilworth's hostility is so well known that the community is bypassed by real estate agents when serving prospective Jewish purchasers." Finally in the 1970s, according to Rubenstein, Kenilworth admitted Jews.[23]

Kenilworth exemplified a national pattern. As the United States went more racist, it also went more anti-Semitic. After 1900, most elite suburbs quickly moved beyond barring blacks to bar Jews, and a few banned Catholics, especially if they were from southern or eastern Europe and looked "swarthy." Here sundown suburbs parted company with independent sundown towns, few of which made a big deal out of religion.[24] Chapter 9 shows how Grosse Pointe, Michigan, also made it difficult or impossible for Jewish families to move in.[25] Some suburbs limited sales to "members of the Aryan branch of the Caucasian race," thereby excluding "Mediterraneans" as well as Jews.

Imagining Jews as a problem pushes this line of thought to the breaking point, because Jews are *not* thought of as problems today, at least not as problems having to do with crime or poor school performance, but during the heyday of eugenics, Jews, like blacks, were thought to be stupid. On the standardized tests that came into vogue during and after World War I—the U.S. Army alpha test, the Stanford-Binet IQ test, and the SAT—Jews from Russia and Eastern Europe did perform poorly compared to WASPs.[26]

Affluent WASP families increasingly viewed living near Jews as a threat to their own social status. Residents of several Boston suburbs reported that their communities formerly kept out Jews. Laura Hobson's bestselling novel, *Gentleman's Agreement,* made Darien, Connecticut, a sundown suburb of New York City, briefly notorious in 1947 when it publicized the town's practice of not letting Jews spend the night. In 1959, the Anti-Defamation League commented on Bronxville, another suburb of New York City:

> The Incorporated Village of Bronxville in Westchester County has earned a reputation for admitting to its precincts as home-owners or -renters only those who profess to be Christians. According to informed observers, this mile-square village, with a population of 6500, does not have any known Jewish families residing within its boundaries. . . . Even in the apartment buildings located in Bronxville there are no known Jewish tenants.

A report on the Midwest by British economist Graham Hutton tells of Jews' precarious situation in that region just after World War II:

> With exceptions in the Midwest today that could almost be named and counted on the fingers of two hands, the Jewish families—at least, those known to be Jews—settled in defined districts and were "restricted" from refined ones. They are still kept out of the select residential districts and clubs and have therefore established their own.

The same pattern held in suburb after suburb, as far west as La Jolla, California. Most upper- and upper-middle-class suburbs kept out Jews, often until well after World War II.[27] Until the 1980s, Jewish Americans were typically confined to just a handful of suburbs. A resident who favored barring Jews gave one reason: "Where [Jews] come in, the niggers follow and knock the property [values] down."[28] Another reason was sheer status: a town or neighborhood was thought to be higher-class if it kept out Jews. This is still true in some parts of the upper class.[29]

Sundown Suburbs Explode After World War II

By the end of World War II, the housing pressure in African American neighborhoods in inner cities was enormous, greater even than the pent-up postwar demand among white families. A 1943 memo of the Illinois Interracial Commission pointed out that 80% of the black population of Chicago was packed into less than 5 square miles, making dwelling units "unbelievably crowded." Paradoxically, while World War II had a salutary effect on race relations in the United States, it also contributed to an explosion in the development of sundown suburbs. Between 1947 and 1967, more towns were established on a whites-only basis than ever before. Almost every suburb that sprang up or expanded after World War II was whites-only. Among the largest were the three Levittowns, in New Jersey, New York, and Pennsylvania, begun in the 1950s. In fact, Levitt & Sons was by far the largest home builder in America after World War II. By one estimate, the firm built 8% of all postwar suburban housing—all of it sundown. As Kenneth Jackson notes, "The Levitt organization . . . publicly and officially refused to sell to blacks for two decades after the war. Nor did resellers deal with minorities." The result—"not surprisingly," in Jackson's words—was that "in 1960 not a single one of the Long Island Levittown's 82,000 residents was black." William Levitt claimed, "Our housing policy has been to abide by local law or custom" when he built his sundown suburbs, but this was not true. The African American family that finally desegregated Levittown, Pennsylvania, moved in from an integrated town only a mile away. Even more disgraceful was his performance in Manhasset, on Long Island: according to journalist Geoffrey Mohan, Levitt used "restrictive covenants to ban Jews from his early Manhasset developments. It was strictly business." Levitt himself not only was Jewish but lived in Manhasset![30]

Even some suburbs now famous for their racial tolerance were all-white by policy at first. Oak Park, which abuts the western edge of Chicago, is now nationally renowned as an integrated community, but it was a sundown suburb in 1950, when the Percy Julian family tried to move in. The Julians could hardly have been more deserving candidates: Dr. Julian earned a doctorate in chemistry from the University of Vienna and synthesized cortisone in 1949; his wife was the first African American woman ever to earn a doctorate in sociology. Recognized for his scientific eminence, Percy Julian had been named Chicagoan of the Year in 1949. None of that helped when the Julians tried to become the first African American family to move into Oak Park. James Hecht, who worked for open housing in Buffalo and Richmond, tells what happened:

> When Dr. Percy L. Julian bought an expensive fifteen-room house in Oak Park in 1950, the color of his skin was more important to many people . . . than the fact that he was one of the nation's leading chemists. The water commissioner refused to turn on the water until the Julians threatened to go to court. There were threats by anonymous telephone callers, and an attempt was made to burn the house down. But Dr. Julian—then the chief of soybean research for the Glidden Company . . . a man known throughout the scientific world for his synthesis of hormones and development of processes for their manufacture—hired private guards and moved into the house.

Thus Oak Park, like Tuxedo Park, not only did not try to enforce fair housing but tried to use its control over access to water to stay all-white.[31]

The degree to which African Americans were simply shut out of the suburban explosion is astonishing. Historian Thomas Sugrue tells that in Detroit, "a mere 1,500 of the 186,000 single-family houses constructed in the metropolitan Detroit area in the 1940s were open to blacks. As late as 1951, only 1.15% of the new homes constructed in the metropolitan Detroit area were available to blacks." Just four African American families entered any of the white suburbs of Chicago in 1961–62 combined. By 1970, exclusion was so complete that fewer than 500 black families lived in white suburban neighborhoods in the entire Chicago metropolitan area, and most of those were in just five or six suburbs. Sociologist Troy Duster cites an even more amazing yet representative statistic: "Of 350,000 new homes built in northern California between 1946 and 1960 with FHA [Federal Housing Administration] support, *fewer than 100 went to blacks.* That same pattern holds for the whole state, and for the nation as well." Just as Palos Verdes Estates had been more segregated than the suburbs closer to Los Angeles, in the late 1950s and early 1960s the suburbs beyond Palos Verdes Estates took the phenomenon one step further, turning the entire Palos Verdes peninsula "into a congerie of walled, privatized residential 'cities,' " in the words of Mike Davis. "Rolling Hills did it, and Rancho Palos Verdes, and then Rolling Hills Estate." Orange

County, the next county out, was worse yet. Statewide, after the legislature passed a fair housing law in 1963, Californians repealed it by voting overwhelmingly for Proposition 14, but the California Supreme Court found this unconstitutional in 1966.[32]

The FHA Helped Create Our Sundown Suburbs

The Federal Housing Administration, set up during the Depression to make it easier for Americans to buy homes, was a large part of the problem. In fact, Charles Abrams, an early proponent of integrated housing, saw the FHA as the most important single cause of residential segregation. He wrote in 1955:

> From its inception the FHA set itself up as the protector of the all white neighborhood. It sent its agents into the field to keep Negroes and other minorities from buying houses in white neighborhoods. It exerted pressure against builders who dared to build for minorities, and against lenders willing to lend on mortgages.

In 1938, the FHA held, "If a neighborhood is to retain stability, it is necessary that its properties shall continue to be occupied by the same social and racial classes." The FHA advocated restrictive covenants, "since these provide the surest protection against undesirable encroachment," and its *Manual* contained a model restrictive covenant until 1948. In that year, assistant FHA commissioner W. J. Lockwood boasted, "The FHA has never insured a housing project of mixed occupancy."[33]

The FHA even engaged in such absurdities as requiring the developer of Mayfair Park, a postwar residential subdivision in South Burlington, Vermont, to include its model racially restrictive covenant in each deed before it would guarantee loans in the development. Scarcely a hundred black families lived in the entire state, so the covenants did not stop any mass influx of African Americans into the suburb. They did, however, make salient to white purchasers that their government believed black families were a danger from which whites required protection, even that far north. Portfolio 29 shows a physical legacy of the FHA's policy, still on the ground in Detroit.[34]

FHA publications repeatedly listed "inharmonious racial or nationality groups" alongside such noxious disamenities as "smoke, odors, and fog." Again, this was the familiar "blacks as the problem" ideology, and the FHA's solution was identical to that employed by independent sundown towns: keep "the problem" out. Palen states that loan guarantees by the FHA and Veterans

Administration (VA) were the most important single cause of postwar suburbanization, and more than 98% of the millions of home loans guaranteed by the FHA and VA after World War II were available only to whites. This was the money that funded the Levittowns and most other postwar sundown suburbs. America became a nation of homeowners largely *after* World War II, in the suburbs. Indeed, more Americans bought single-family homes in the decade after the war than in the previous 150 years, according to historian Lizabeth Cohen. African Americans were thus not only shut out of the suburbs but also kept from participating in Americans' surest route to wealth accumulation, federally subsidized home ownership. Federal support for home ownership not only included the FHA and VA programs but also the mortgage interest tax deduction, which made home ownership in the suburbs cheaper than apartment rental in the cities—for whites. Housing prices then skyrocketed, tripling in the 1970s alone; this appreciation laid the groundwork for the astonishing 1-to-11 black-to-white wealth ratio that now afflicts African American families.[35]

When the federal government did spend money on black housing, it funded the opposite of suburbia: huge federally assisted high-rise "projects" concentrated in the inner city. We are familiar with the result, which now seems natural to us, market-driven: African Americans living near the central business district and whites living out in the suburbs. Actually, locating low-income housing on cheaper, already vacant land in the suburbs would have been more natural, more market-driven. One of Chicago's most notorious housing projects, Cabrini Green, lies just a stone's throw west of an expensive and desirable lakefront neighborhood north of the Loop, separated by the elevated railroad tracks. This is costly land. To justify its price, the Chicago Housing Authority had to pile hundreds of units onto the tract, building poorly devised physical structures that bred a festering, unsafe social structure. The steps taken by suburban developers and governments to be all-white were interferences in the housing market that kept African Americans from buying homes and locked them in overwhelmingly black tracts inside the city.

Too Little, Too Late

In 1968, the federal government finally switched sides. Sympathetic reaction to the assassination of Dr. Martin Luther King Jr. gave Congress the political will to pass Title VIII of the Civil Rights Act of 1968. Often called the Fair Housing Act, this law prohibits racial discrimination in the sale, rental, and financing of housing. Also in 1968, the Supreme Court in *Jones v. Mayer* required "all housing, with no exception, open without regard to race, at least as a matter of legal right," in the words of W. A. Low and V. A. Clift. However, enforcement was left up "to litigation by persons discriminated against." The 1968 act also did not make the profound difference that its supporters expected, again owing to problems with enforcement. It was left to the victims, or perhaps the Department of Justice on their behalf, to enforce the law by litigation; the department that was supposed to enforce it, Housing and Urban Development (HUD), had no enforcement powers.[36]

Sociologist Douglas Massey tells the result very simply: "Discrimination went underground." In suburbs across the nation, gentlemen's agreements now came to the fore. It was "understood," there was a "gentleman's agreement," so no one had to say a word. Steering, lying, stalling, special requirements imposed on blacks, missed appointments, wrong addresses—all were used to shut out African American would-be home buyers.[37] Michael Danielson quoted a study of racial exclusion in the San Francisco Bay Area: "Every routine act [in buying a home], every bit of ritual in the sale or rental of a dwelling unit can be performed in a way calculated to make it either difficult or impossible to consummate a deal." For example, according to David Freund, "the courts did not ban the use of race-specific language in appraisal manuals until the late 1970s."[38]

The 1968 act and *Jones v. Mayer* did prompt some residential integration, at least by the 1990s. Unfortunately, open housing came too late, after suburbia was largely built. Across the United States, whites had kept African Americans out of most suburbs throughout most of the twentieth century. By 1968, suburbs were labeled racially. Once in place, these reputations were self-sustaining. Desegregating them was an uphill struggle, a mountain that we are still climbing. Like anyone else, African Americans don't want to live in a place where they aren't wanted, and one way to deduce that they aren't wanted is to note that no African Americans live there. Today, just a little steering by realtors suffices to keep sundown suburbs nearly all-white. Here is an example from Pennsylvania. Whites and blacks refer to the suburbs across the Susquehanna River from Harrisburg as "the white shore." A man who grew up there wrote me:

I can tell you that there were (are?) sundown towns in Central Pennsylvania. You were right about the "white shore." I have no objective proof at all. However my mother grew up in Enola, and my uncle lived in Camp Hill. It was common knowledge that African-Americans would not be sold a house in those towns and those that surrounded them. It was indeed a "white shore."

By August 2002, when a new black employee moved to Harrisburg to take up her new job with the State of Pennsylvania, the pattern was in place. "The realtor told me I could live on the west shore, but it's really called 'the *white* shore,' so I'd probably be happier somewhere else." She bought in Harrisburg. Such steering is illegal, but it goes on every day.[39]

African Americans still have trouble getting equal treatment at each step of the home-buying process, according to speakers at a 2003 conference in Washington, D.C., subtitled "New Evidence on Housing Discrimination." Speakers presented data to show that in most suburbs of all social classes, realtors, lenders, and other parties to housing sales continue to discriminate covertly against African Americans, although the differences in treatment were not dramatic. In 2003, Shanna Smith, head of the National Fair Housing Alliance, summed up the problem: "The government is not serious about fair housing enforcement. If they were, they would fund it."[40]

As a result, African Americans remain markedly underrepresented in suburbs, and to the degree they do live in suburbia, they are overconcentrated in just a few suburbs. Nationally, in 1950, African Americans occupied 4.6% of all housing units outside central cities but still within metropolitan areas. By 1970, that proportion had actually dropped to 4.2%. Baltimore County, for example, a suburban jurisdiction to the east, north, and west of Baltimore, doubled in population during that interval. Meanwhile, the number of African Americans never budged, so the proportion of African Americans in the Baltimore suburbs fell from 7% to 3%.[41]

Even those small percentages were artificially inflated. Geographer Harold Rose points out that most "suburban" African Americans live in three types of towns:

- Historically black towns and townships[42]
- Independent industrial towns that then became part of a metropolitan area, such as Chester, Pennsylvania, or Pontiac, Michigan
- Older inner suburbs, contiguous to the city itself, that had become majority-black as early as 1970, such as East Orange, New Jersey (Newark); Seat Pleasant, Maryland (Washington); East Cleveland, Ohio (Cleveland); Hamtramck, Michigan (Detroit); University City, Missouri (St. Louis); and Inglewood, California (Los Angeles)

The first two categories have little in common with what most Americans mean by "suburbia" but account for many "black suburbanites."[43]

The concentration of African Americans into a handful of suburbs is striking in many metropolitan areas. "Long Island has the most racially isolated and segregated suburbs in the nation," according to reporter Michael Powell, writing in 2002. About 10% of Long Island's population is African American, but "almost all black residents are bunched into a dozen or so towns, from Roosevelt to Hempstead, Wyandanch, and Uniondale." Meanwhile, two-thirds of Long Island's municipalities remained less than 1% black, and half of those had no black residents at all. In northern New Jersey in 1970, 89% of Essex County's 72,000 African Americans lived in three towns—East Orange, Orange, and Montclair. Meanwhile, only 7 African Americans lived in Roseland and 8 in Fairfield. By 2000, 327,000 African Americans lived in Essex County; East Orange and Orange had gone majority-black; but just 65 African Americans lived in Roseland and Fairfield combined. Similarly, 80% of the African Americans in Oakland County, north of Detroit, lived in just three cities.[44]

Chicago follows the same pattern. In the 1960s, all of the African Americans who moved to the suburbs, 51,000 people, went to just 15 of 237 suburbs, according to Danielson. These 15 suburbs had 83% of Chicago's 128,300 suburban African Americans. Three of these—Harvey, Ford Heights, and Robbins—were overwhelmingly black and ranked among the poorest suburbs in the nation. Meanwhile, all other Chicago suburbs remained overwhelmingly white. By 1980, of Chicago's 285 suburbs, 9 had populations 30 to 50% black, while 117 were less than 1% black. "It is evident that those racial housing patterns didn't develop by accident," wrote Arthur Hayes in *Black Enterprise*. A study of suburban Chicago in 1993 demonstrated what Meyer called "the tenacity of segregation." Only 423 African Americans were among the 183,000 denizens of McHenry County, about 0.2% African Americans made up more than 10% of the population of Will County, but three-fourths of them lived in just three communities. Kane County was 5.8% African American in 2000, but nearly 96% of those black residents lived in just two towns, Aurora and Elgin.[45]

Sundown suburbs are the key reason why geographer Jeff Crump was able to maintain that "cities in the United States are the most racially segregated urban areas in the world." The normal processes of the marketplace would result in a sprinkling of African Americans everywhere, albeit with some areas of greater concentration, like the distribution of, say, Italian Americans.[46]

The next chapter explores the underlying reasons why towns and suburbs went sundown in the first place.

PART III

The Sociology of Sundown Towns

6

Underlying Causes

One of the most striking aspects of racial segregation in 1993 is the national sense that it is inescapable.

—John C. Boger, "Toward Ending Residential Segregation," 1993[1]

THIS CHAPTER SEEKS ANSWERS to important "why" questions, the most basic of which is: Why have African Americans been particularly targeted for exclusion? Other key questions are: Why did thousands of towns and counties across America go sundown? What caused a town to expel its African Americans or resolve never to let any in? Why did another town, a few miles down the road, always allow African Americans to live in it? What predicts which suburbs opened to African Americans when most remained closed?

Why African Americans?

We have seen that sundown towns did not always direct their exclusionary policies against African Americans but sometimes drove out or prohibited Chinese, Japanese, Jewish, Native, or Mexican Americans. For shorter periods, a few towns kept out Greeks, Sicilians, or other European ethnic minorities. Still other towns drove out or excluded Mormons, homosexuals, labor union members, and perhaps Seventh Day Adventists.[2] Nevertheless, African Americans have been excluded much more universally than any other group.[3] Although a few Western counties did exclude Chinese Americans, none did so after 1970. I know of no county that ever prohibited any other group countywide. Indeed, after about 1970, few sundown towns or suburbs kept out any minority other than African Americans.

Why?

The answer to this last question *seems* to be that African Americans differ more from whites physically: in color, features, and general appearance. On reflection, however, this is not so obvious. Neither skin color in itself, nor aesthetics, nor physical characteristics explain racism. History does. Events and processes in American history from the time of slavery to the present explain why we think it "natural" to differentiate based on skin color. In his important book *Minority Education and Caste*, anthropologist John Ogbu observed that historically, European Americans systematically subjugated three groups: Native Americans, Mexican Americans, and African Americans, taking the land of the first two and the labor of the third. As part of the process of justifying American history, European Americans have therefore systematically stigmatized these groups as inferior. That's why Ogbu called Native Americans, Mexican Americans, and African Americans our "caste minorities," which he differentiated from other "voluntary minorities."[4]

Among these three caste minorities, whites encountered African Americans *primarily* as slaves for almost 250 years—from 1619 through at least 1863. To be sure, whites enslaved some Native Americans, but the most common encounters between European Americans and Native Americans were not master-to-slave. Even less was this true between Anglos and Mexicans. White racism therefore became first and foremost a rationale for African slavery. That is why America's *"real* non-whites," if you will, have for centuries been its African Americans. Ultimately, then, even after it ended, slavery was responsible for the continuing stigmatizing of African Americans, expressed in their exclusion from sundown towns, among other ways. Even today, whites feel most strongly about differentiating themselves from African Americans, not Jewish, Mexican,[5] Native, or Asian Americans.

The Nadir Made Sundown Towns Possible

Answering the other questions—why did so many towns go sundown? what caused one town to do so but not another?—is not so easy. It is always hard to assign causes for large-scale historical movements, and all the more so when the movement entails attitudes and actions that are embarrassing or repugnant in retrospect. I suggest two kinds of underlying factors were at work. First, the spirit of the times—the zeitgeist—changed. I am referring to the deepening racism known as the Nadir of race relations, of course, between 1890 and 1940. This change in our national culture affected towns all across America. But it did not affect them equally. The second type of underlying social and cultural causes predisposed some towns—but not others—to go sundown. These factors included a Democratic voting majority, mono-ethnic makeup, and strong labor movement. Such characteristics did not determine that a town would go sundown, but as the Nadir deepened, African Americans in these towns lived on the knife edge. The actions of a few individuals on one side or the other often swayed the outcome. Even chance played a role.

Chapter 2 analyzed how and why racism intensified after 1890 across the United States. Lynchings rose to their all-time high, the Ku Klux Klan was reborn as a national institution, and whites drove blacks from occupation after occupation. Causal factors underlying the Nadir included the three *i*'s— Indian wars, increasing opposition to immigrants, and imperialism—as well as the rise of Social Darwinism to justify the opulence of the Gilded Age. Of course, the racism that had arisen earlier in our culture as a rationale for slavery was always a key underlying ingredient.

If not for this intensification of white supremacy between 1890 and 1940, towns and suburbs across the North would never have been allowed to expel and exclude African Americans and others. The most obvious way that the Nadir of race relations gave birth to sundown towns was in the changed response of governments when whites drove out African Americans. Two incidents in Anna, in southern Illinois, one before the Nadir and one during it, highlight its impact. This book began with a mention of the 1909 lynching that led to the expulsion of African Americans from Anna; Chapter 7 tells that story in detail. But 1909 was not the first expulsion of African Americans from Anna-Jonesboro, which had long been anti-black. In 1862, citizens of Union County had supported a new state constitutional provision, "No Negro or Mulatto shall migrate or settle in this state," by a vote of 1,583 to 98. Complaining because ex-slaves passed through the county going north on the Illinois Central Rail Road, the Anna newspaper editor wrote, "We have laws prohibiting their settlement here." During the Civil War, Cairo was a place of refuge for African Americans from the Lower Mississippi Valley. United States Army officers struggled to cope with the flood of refugees. In 1863, residents in and around Cobden, six miles north of Anna, agreed to take some of these men and women as workers in their apple orchards. Benjamin Fenton brought in about 40 African American refugees to work on his farm. Whites from the Anna-Jonesboro area charged the orchard owners with "unlawfully and willfully bringing [slaves] into the State of Illinois . . . in order to free them," a violation of the old statewide racial exclusion law passed before the Civil War. Then a mob of about 25 men led by an Anna doctor visited Fenton and forced him to return his workers to Cairo.[6]

After the Anna mob drove the African American farmworkers from Union County in 1863, the army commander at Cairo who had let them go there in the first place was outraged. He wrote that he would have sent armed troops to protect them if the farmer who employed them had requested it. The military later arrested the mob leaders and imprisoned them for most of the rest of the war.

But when Anna whites again drove out their black population in 1909, no one was ever arrested. The federal government did nothing; neither did the state. Indeed, the times had shifted so much that there was no thought that either government *might* intervene. Although the increasing racism of the Nadir was a necessary characteristic underlying the outbreak of sundown towns, it cannot explain why one town went sundown while another did not. In Union County, for instance, the Nadir cannot explain why Anna drove out its African Americans in 1909 and has kept them out ever since, while Cobden, five miles north, has African American households to this day.[7]

Tautological "Causes"

Most residents of sundown towns and counties are of little help when asked why their town has been all-white for so long. They don't know about the Nadir, and few ever think about the underlying causes of their town's racial policy. Instead, local historians often offer tautological or nonsensical "explanations" for their town's absence of African Americans. Typically these alleged factors have nothing to do with race. Before planting the seedlings of the real causes, I need to clear out the underbrush of erroneous reasons that many people give to explain all-white communities.

The spokesman for a historical society in a Pennsylvania county "explained" its all-white demography with this sentence: "Most or all of our towns were white because the area attracted few blacks." The argument is airtight, of course, but circular. "There's never been much need for them" is another favorite—but how an area's "need" for new settlers comes with a racial label goes unexplained. "There wasn't work for what skills they had," said a local history expert from another Pennsylvania county whose white population between 1900 and 1940 was mostly farmers and miners. But mining and farming were precisely the occupations engaged in by most African American men.

The flip side of the "lack of jobs" theory is the notion that African Americans went to big cities because that's where the jobs were. "There were more jobs in Milwaukee," said several Wisconsin residents, trying to explain the increasing whiteness of midsized Wisconsin towns during the first half of the twentieth century. But "jobs in the cities" likewise fails as a cause of sundown towns. Of course, Milwaukee *does* have more jobs than any other Wisconsin city, but there were jobs aplenty in smaller Wisconsin cities such as Appleton, Fond du Lac, and Oshkosh, in the four counties surrounding Lake Winnebago. Indeed, those counties were urbanizing between 1890 and 1930. Precisely as their black population declined by 78%, their white population increased by 45%, from 149,514 to 216,143. Similarly, from 1900 to 1970, Granite City, Illinois, zoomed in population from 3,122 to 40,440, owing to skyrocketing employment, while its black population fell from 154 to 6. Obviously these growing cities had an abundance of new jobs—for whites.

As well, it is important to understand that most jobs in big cities were flatly closed to African Americans throughout the Nadir. Breweries in Milwaukee started to hire African Americans only in 1950, the city did not employ a single black teacher until 1951, and its first major department store to hire an African American as a full-time sales clerk did not do so until 1952. In northern cities, most jobs in construction were reserved for whites until the 1970s. So big-city jobs weren't much of a draw, except in a few cities such as Detroit and Pittsburgh, where a sizable fraction of industrial jobs were open to African Americans.[8]

The claim that lack of jobs caused towns to go all-white is rendered preposterous by those sundown towns where African Americans have been allowed to work but not to live. African Americans helped build Hoover Dam but had to commute from Las Vegas to do it, while white workers and their families lived in Boulder City, a sundown town built just for them. African Americans helped build Kentucky Dam, but after they finished, their housing—"Negro Village"—was razed, they were booted out, and Marshall County, Kentucky, resumed being a sundown county. Today African Americans commute from Hayti Heights, Missouri, to work in Paragould, Arkansas; from Peoria, Illinois, to Pekin; and from Mattoon, Illinois, to Effingham. African Americans care for patients at the Illinois State [Mental] Hospital in Anna but live in Cairo and Cobden. Sundown towns such as Cullman, Alabama, and Herrin, Illinois, have long been serviced during the day by domestics from nearby African American "townships." Ford Motor Company located its largest single plant in Dearborn, Michigan, a sundown suburb; thousands of African American car builders commuted to it every day from Detroit. In 1956, *U.S. News and World Report* estimated that "at least 15,000 Negroes" worked in Dearborn but were "barred, completely and semiofficially," from living there. More thousands commuted to a huge General Motors plant in neighboring Warren but had to return home to Detroit when night fell. In 1972, 4,353 African Americans worked in Livonia, another sundown suburb of Detroit, but could not live there. "Lack of jobs" can hardly explain the absence of African Americans from any independent town such as Paragould or multiclass suburb such as Dearborn in which they work but do not live, because these towns house *white* workers who do the same jobs.[9]

Even more blatant have been those sundown towns that allowed African American laborers to sojourn in temporary housing on construction sites for the summer construction season but would not let them stay once the season was over. In fact, using lack of jobs to explain black absence often gets the causation directly backward. In 1943, the chairman of Illinois's Inter-Racial Commission noted, "Many plants in towns where Negroes are not permitted to reside, give that as an excuse for not hiring Negroes."[10]

Some theories emphasize social isolation: why *should* African Americans move into out-of-the-way hamlets distant from centers of African American population? In short, the lack of blacks was just "natural," or resulted from historical coincidence. I began my research with this hypothesis—that most all-white towns never *happened* to draw any black residents—but it didn't hold up. Another near-tautology lurks: African Americans didn't move in because few African Americans lived there to attract them. Before 1890, however, African Americans moved to counties and towns throughout America, as Table 1 showed (page 56)—even to isolated places such as northern Maine, northern Wisconsin, and Idaho north of the Snake River Valley. Then during the Great Retreat, they withdrew to the larger cities and a mere handful of small towns. Distance from the South, from African American population centers, or from major trade routes cannot explain this pattern, because towns in Maine, Wisconsin, Idaho, and elsewhere were at least as isolated socially between 1865 and 1890, when African Americans were moving into them, as they were between 1890 and 1930, when African Americans were fleeing them.[11] In other words, because social isolation cannot explain the *increases* in black population in northern counties before 1890, it cannot explain why those increases reversed after that date. Something different went on after 1890.

Sundown Suburbs Are Not "Natural" and Not Due to Class

Social isolation has even been used to explain overwhelmingly white suburbs: whites have imagined that African Americans prefer the excitement of the big city to such suburban values as home ownership, peace and quiet, tree-lined streets, and good school systems. This notion is absurd, as historian Andrew

Wiese showed in 2004. Wiese summarized survey research as far back as the 1940s, finding no support for this stereotype. Among a sample of six hundred middle-income black families in New York City in 1948, for example, nine out of ten wanted to buy their own homes, and three in four wanted to move to suburbia. Many African American families have the same fervent desire for a patch of ground that white suburbanites manifest.[12]

Other whites seem to think it's somehow "natural" for blacks to live in the inner city, whites in the outer suburbs. This idea is a component of what law professor John Boger calls "the national sense that [residential segregation] is inescapable." Most African Americans arrived by train, goes this line of thought, and they're just taking a long time to move out from the vicinity of the train station; as soon as they make enough money, they too will move to the suburbs. But the whiteness of our suburbs is not "natural."[13]

Over and over, white academics as well as residents of sundown suburbs suggest that social class explained sundown suburbs, if not independent sundown towns. "*I* couldn't live in Grosse Pointe either," one professor put it in 2002, referring to one of Detroit's richest suburbs, also one of its whitest. For all-white suburbs to result from classism is seen as defensible, because classism is OK, since we all presumably have a reasonable if not equal chance to get into the upper class. This ideology is a form of Social Darwinism: the best people wind up on top, and whites are smarter, better students, work harder at their jobs, etc. People who think like this don't see Grosse Pointe's whiteness as a white problem but as a black problem. "They" haven't worked hard enough, etc., so they haven't accumulated enough wealth—and perhaps enough social connections and knowledge—to crack these suburbs.

This line of thought seems plausible. Segregation by class *is* an important component of suburbanization, and increasingly so. Residents of elite suburbs such as Grosse Pointe segregate on the basis of both race and class, and for the same reason: being distant from African Americans and from lower-class people conveys status.[14] Nevertheless, the reasoning does not hold up, for two reasons. First, it ignores history. People who think like this have no idea that as recently as the 1960s and 1970s, when today's mature adults were starting their careers, whites in much of the country flatly banned African Americans as a group from many occupations—not just professions but also jobs like construction work, department store clerk, flight attendant, and railroad engineer.

Second, sundown suburbs simply do not result from class. Research by Michael Danielson points to a key flaw in the argument: the proportion of a metropolitan area's blacks in a suburb, *controlling for income,* is less than half the proportion of whites in that suburb, except for the handful of interracial suburbs. That is, if we tried to guess the number of African Americans in a suburb just using income, we would always predict more than twice as many black people as actually lived there. Something has been keeping them out in addition to their class status. Conversely, a much higher proportion of poor white families live in suburbs, compared to poor black families. If income were the crucial factor, then there would be little difference by race in the distribution of the poor.[15]

Continuing with our Grosse Pointe example, in the Detroit metropolitan area, class has mattered even less, race even more, than elsewhere in the nation, according to research by Karl Taeuber. "More than half of the white families in each income level, from very poor to very rich, lived in the suburbs," he found. "Among blacks, only one-tenth of the families at each income level (including very rich) lived in the suburbs." In short, *social class, at least as measured by income, made little difference in the level of suburbanization.* Rich whites have been much more suburban than rich blacks; poor whites have been much more suburban than poor blacks.[16]

Sundown suburbs with an industrial base—such as Dearborn, Warren, and Livonia, around Detroit—have long employed African Americans, at least as janitors, but they could not spend the night. Some of these suburbs—like Livonia and Warren—are working-class. Other sundown suburbs, like independent sundown towns, are multiclass: houses in Dearborn, in 1997, ranged from starter homes around $45,000 to executive homes for $800,000 and up. Social class simply cannot explain the absence of African Americans from multiclass or working-class communities. Nor can it explain the absence of Jews from such elite suburbs as Kenilworth and Flossmoor, Illinois, and Darien, Connecticut.[17]

Sociologist Reynolds Farley and his associates used our old friend D, the Index of Dissimilarity, to compare the power of race to that of class. Specifically regarding Detroit, they observed, "If household income alone determined where people lived, the Index of Dissimilarity would be 15 [almost completely integrated] instead of 88 [almost completely segregated]." Instead,

> Economic criteria account for little of the observed concentration of blacks in central cities and their relative absence from the suburbs. The current level of residential segregation must be attributed largely to action and attitudes, past and present, which have restricted the entry of blacks into predominately white neighborhoods.[18]

Indeed, blaming the whiteness of elite sundown suburbs on their wealth actually reverses the causality of caste and class. It is mostly the other way around: racial and religious exclusion came first, not class. Suburbs that kept out blacks and Jews became more prestigious, so they attracted the very rich. The absence of African Americans itself became a selling point, which in turn helped these suburbs become so affluent because houses there commanded higher prices. To this day, all-white suburbs attract the very rich. Twelve of the communities on *Worth* magazine's list of 50 richest towns were all-white in 2000 or had just one or two African American families. Typically they were all-white first and became rich only when affluent families moved in. After 1959, for example, when Jews were let into La Jolla, California, a number of WASP families fled from La Jolla to Rancho Santa Fe, fifteen miles north and inland from the beach. Now Rancho Santa Fe is #16 on *Worth*'s list, well above La Jolla at #85,[19] based on median home price.[20]

In yet another way, blaming blacks for being poor, as a cause of segregation, reverses cause and effect. As Chapter 12 shows, residential segregation itself constrains and diminishes the cultural capital and social connections of African Americans, thus artificially decreasing their income and wealth. It won't do to then use blacks' lower income and wealth to explain residential segregation.

Other Nonsensical "Causes"

Related to the isolation hypothesis is climate. A historical society leader in western Maryland explained why Garrett County had only a handful of African Americans when all other Maryland counties had at least a thousand: "It's too cold here." Whites "know" that African Americans don't like cold weather, which "explains" why they didn't move to a given northern town or county. Persons making this claim have obviously never been to Detroit, where African Americans outnumber European Americans three to one, yet winter punishes anyone not prepared for its rigors. Garrett County is hardly colder than Detroit—hardly colder in 2002, for that matter, when I had the conversation, than it had been in 1890, when it had 185 African Americans. The fact that the very next county to the east had more than 1,000 African Americans, while Garrett County had at most one black household, is a dead giveaway. Such abrupt disparities can only result from different racial policies, not from factors such as climate.[21]

Counties in Maine or Wisconsin were also no warmer in 1865–90, when African Americans were moving into them, than in 1890–1940, when they were moving out. Moreover, African Americans returned to most Wisconsin all-white towns between 1970 and 1990. Manitowoc, a sundown town that had just 2 African Americans in 1970, had 71 by 1990, and Oshkosh had a whopping 435 (approaching 1% of its total population). The migration of African Americans to towns throughout Wisconsin after 1970, like their earlier arrival before 1890, underscores that something other than isolation or climate was required to force their departure between 1890 and 1940. Global warming to the contrary, Wisconsin winters did not turn noticeably warmer after 1970, when blacks were again moving into formerly all-white counties and towns across the state.

Also related to isolation is the claim that independent sundown towns are miserable backwaters. "Who would *want* to live there?" a white professor at Texas A & M University in Commerce suggested in 1999, referring to Cumby, a small nearby sundown town. "What a dump!" A white woman from Buffalo said, "There's nothing there!" referring to nearby Tonawanda and North Tonawanda. To be sure, some sundown towns *are* small, isolated, and backward—hardly the stars to which rational Americans of any race would hitch their wagons. Cumby, for example, *is* a dump. Moreover, during the twentieth century Americans of all races did migrate to cities, which they believed offered cultural as well as educational and economic opportunities lacking in small towns. Nevertheless, even to explain why towns as small, isolated, and backward as Cumby have *no* African Americans, "small, isolated, and backward" won't do, because humans are unpredictable. People are always moving into and out of small towns in America, even into dying towns, for all kinds of reasons. So would African Americans if given a chance. Indeed, so *did* African Americans between 1865 and 1890 and, in those places whose exclusionary policies have cracked, between 1980 or 1990 and 2005. The "backwater" explanation is rarely offered by residents of a town itself, because it puts down their town and because they know that it isn't so bad that a family has to be irrational to move into it.[22]

Amazingly, I have heard this explanation given for whole regions—the Ozarks, straddling the Missouri-Arkansas line for nearly 300 miles; the Cumberland Plateau in eastern Tennessee and Kentucky; the Texas and Oklahoma panhandles; large swaths of southern Illinois and southern Indiana; the Upper Peninsula of Michigan; and parts of Appalachia. "Who would want to live there, anyway?" But implying that African Americans have been making rational unconstrained choices to avoid such towns won't do, because they haven't been.[23] Their choices have been constrained. Indeed, many of the people who supply these explanations do know that the place under discussion has kept out African Americans by policy. They put down the town or even the region not really to explain its whiteness but merely to make it seem a problem not worth fixing.

Moreover, backwater isolation certainly wasn't judged adequate by whites who lived in such isolated little towns as Cumby, or De Land or Villa Grove, Illinois. They never relied on their towns' smallness, backwardness, or remoteness from black population centers to "protect" themselves from African Americans, instead taking care to pass ordinances, blow whistles, or engage in other acts, formal or informal, to keep them out. Furthermore, many all-white towns are not isolated. Some are on important transportation routes, including Effingham, Illinois, or Tonawanda, New York. Some are themselves important manufacturing or educational centers, such as Appleton, Wisconsin; Niles, Ohio; or Norman, Oklahoma. Isolation and happenstance make even less sense as explanations for sundown suburbs, because some of America's whitest suburbs grew up right next to some of our blackest cities.

All of these tautological and nonsensical "causes"—lack of skills, lack of jobs, social isolation, "natural," social class, climate, avoidance of backwaters—share two characteristics. First, they minimize the problem. Second, they let white society off the hook for it, relying instead on individual choices by African Americans. In recent years, some social scientists, such as Abigail and Stephan Thernstrom, have increasingly relied upon individual decisions by African American families to explain America's intractable residential segregation. Blacks don't want to live in an ocean of white faces, goes the reasoning. If we stop to think, however, sundown towns and suburbs cannot possibly result from decisions by people of color who happily choose to live in black neighborhoods. For there would always be at least *a few* African Americans who would choose to live in majority-white neighborhoods, for some of the same reasons whites do: better schooling, nicer parks, investment value, and social status, in the case of elite suburbs. Others would move for convenience—some African Americans who care for patients in the mental hospital in Anna, Illinois, for example, might choose to live there. Still others would wind up in formerly white towns owing simply to the vagaries of fortune. Voluntary choice simply *cannot* explain what kept sundown towns and suburbs *so* white for so many decades. Some underlying historical and sociological causes do. We will explore three: political ideology, white ethnic solidarity, and labor strife.[24]

Political Ideology as a Cause of Sundown Towns

From its inception, the Democratic Party was "the White Man's Party." Today it is hard for Americans to understand how racist the Democrats became during the Nadir, especially since the two parties flipflopped on this issue beginning in 1964. Historian Nicole Etcheson writes that midwestern Democrats supported what Chief Justice Taney said about black rights in *Dred Scott*: "that they had no rights which the white man was bound to respect." Some Republicans believed African Americans should have all the rights of citizenship, while others, including Abraham Lincoln, were "not, nor ever have been in favor of making voters or jurors of Negroes," as Lincoln put it in Charleston, Illinois, in 1858. As the Civil War progressed, Republican thinking about African Americans moved toward full equality. Democrats underwent no such ideological advance.[25]

In the Midwest I found a striking correlation between counties or towns voting Democratic in the 1850s and driving out their African Americans half a century later. Almost every town on the Illinois River, for example, which stretches diagonally across Illinois from the Mississippi near St. Louis northeast toward Chicago, voted for the Democratic candidate for president in 1868, except for Peoria. The same voting pattern held from at least 1856 to 1892. Between 1890 and 1930, almost every town along the river went sundown, except for Peoria. Why? The Illinois River valley was settled mostly by Democrats from Kentucky and Tennessee. Many of them were exceptionally racist to begin with, having left Kentucky and Tennessee to avoid both slavery and black people. Being a Democrat played a still greater role, owing to the continuing racism expressed by candidates of the Democratic Party.

We can see this same pattern of white supremacy in county histories. In every county along the Illinois River from the Mississippi River to LaSalle-Peru except one, local histories tell of substantial pro-Confederate sentiment during the Civil War. Moreover, treatments of the Civil War in these county histories, whether written in the late nineteenth century or as late as the 1980s, display a white perspective: they rarely mention slavery and say nothing about African Americans. Peoria, the largest city on the Illinois River, is the exception. The rhetoric in its late-nineteenth-century histories is profoundly different, even abolitionist. An 1880 Peoria history tells how midwestern farmers ignored slavery in the 1850s: "Immediately surrounded with peace and tranquility, they paid but little attention to the rumored plots and plans of those who lived and grew rich from the sweat and toil, and blood and flesh of others—aye, even trafficked in the offspring of their own loins." Histories in Democratic counties would never use such language.[26]

Public history as displayed on the landscape shows the same pattern. Peoria dedicated a large Civil War monument shortly after the war ended. Thirty thousand people attended, and the 1880 account of the monument tells how it "would commemorate for all time the names of . . . the men who gave their lives in defense of the Union and of human rights." In Democratic counties, "defense of the Union" would rarely be conjoined with "human rights." Peorians put up another Civil War monument a few years later in Springdale Cemetery, proclaiming "Liberty / Justice / Equality / Pro Patria." Equality would never secure a place on the landscape in a Democratic county.

So it should come as no surprise that during the Nadir, every town on the river *except Peoria*,[27] from the hamlets of Calhoun County all the way up to LaSalle-Peru, drove out or kept out African Americans.

Towns in other parts of Illinois show the same relationship. When Anna-Jonesboro expelled its black population in 1909, political background played a key role. Anna and Jonesboro were overwhelmingly Democratic, while Cobden was partly Republican. During the Civil War, Union County Democrats meeting in Jonesboro adopted a resolution protesting "the introduction of the Negro into our midst" and citing "with apprehension the dangers of robber and violence" to be expected from such an addition to the community. So the 1909 expulsion of African Americans from Anna-Jonesboro was neither novel nor surprising. Nor was Cobden's relative tolerance.

In central Illinois, Mattoon was Republican, in contrast to the next town to the northwest, Sullivan, seat of Moultrie County, highly Democratic. That political difference in 1860 translated to a high level of anti-black sentiment many decades later. Moultrie County had "a few families of the colored race" in 1880, according to an 1881 history, but only one African American was left by 1920. In the 1920s, the KKK burned crosses in Sullivan. Later, according to one oral history report, Sullivan wound up with a sign that read "Nigger, Don't Let The Sun Set On Your Ass." Mattoon, while no race relations haven, has had a stable African American community for many decades.[28]

This pattern—Republican areas in the 1850s remaining interracial in the Nadir, Democratic areas going all white—was not just true for Illinois. It held throughout the North, including California and Oregon.

To be sure, since Democrats called themselves "the White Man's Party," it is somewhat tautological to cite Democratic voting majorities as a cause of white supremacy, rather than as simply another manifestation of it. But not wholly. Americans were Democrats for many reasons, not just the party's racism, just as today Americans are Republicans for many reasons, not just the party's racism. Once an individual became a Democrat, however, perhaps owing to such nonracist reasons as attractive local leaders, one's ethnic group membership, or the Republicans' increasing support for Prohibition, it was hard not to become more racist. After all, the party's songs, speeches, and platform positions usually included attacks on African Americans, along with charges that Republicans favored black rights up to and including "miscegenation," a word coined by Democratic politicos in 1863.

A Different Pattern in the Upland South: Many Unionist Areas Later Expelled African Americans

Political ideology played quite a different role in the South. Politically, the traditional South had been split between Democrats and Whigs in 1850, but with the disintegration of the Whig Party, it became more Democratic, and overwhelmingly so as the South seceded. But Democrats in the traditional South, where slavery had been strong, did not try to drive African Americans out. Instead, they made money off their labor.[29]

The South also had areas, large and small—especially in the hills and mountains, where slaves were few—that tried to stay with the Union.[30] After the war, many of these Unionist areas voted Republican. Until the 1890s, they maintained fairly good relations with their small African American populations, partly because African Americans and white Republicans were political allies. In states where the Republican Party collapsed after the end of Reconstruction, some of these whites then supported third-party movements such as the Readjusters in Virginia, the Union Labor Party in Arkansas, and the Populist Party across all the southern and border states, again usually allied with black voters. After 1890 however, the nationwide tide of increasing white supremacy lapped at the valleys and mountains of the upland South. Like African Americans in Democratic towns in the Midwest and West, African Americans in these formerly Unionist or Republican areas now lived on a knife edge. Their town or county might go either way. Many went sundown.

What happened to cause this shift? Between 1890 and 1910, it became increasingly clear that interracial political coalitions would no longer be viable in the South. Since neither the federal executive nor the Supreme Court did anything to interfere with the "Mississippi Plan" for disfranchising African Americans "legally," other states passed new constitutions emulating Mississippi's between 1890 and 1907. Now white Republicans, Readjusters, Populists, or other anti-Democratic factions had no black counterparts with whom to ally. Democrats also used violence to demonstrate that they would no longer permit blacks or Republicans to hold political office; the coup d'état in Wilmington, North Carolina, in 1898 provided final proof. Now no politics was possible in the South outside the Democratic Party. The "solid South" would not really break until after the 1965 Voting Rights Act undid the disfranchisement of the Nadir period.

What were whites in the nontraditional South to do? In the newly solid South it would not pay to be anything but a Democrat. Allied with this Democratic resurgence, a wave of Confederate nationalism swept the southern and border states beginning shortly before 1890. No longer were Confederate leaders such as Jefferson Davis viewed with ambivalence, having led the South to defeat. Now they were seen as heroes. Now, indeed, the Confederate South had won—if not on the issue of secession, then on the matter of white supremacy. Now Confederate memorials went up across the South, even in counties in the nontraditional South that had not supported secession in 1860. In western Virginia and North Carolina, east Tennessee, northern Georgia and Alabama, north Texas, and much of Arkansas and Missouri, many formerly pro-Unionist whites changed their ideology to join this wave, now the winning side, often becoming hyper-Confederate and anti-black in the process.

At the same time, a new type of Democratic politician arose who professed to be pro-worker and pro-farmer, seemed not to be a tool of the aristocracy, and was rabidly anti-black. Jeff Davis in Arkansas (no relation to Jefferson Davis) was one example, as was James K. Vardaman in Mississippi and Benjamin "Pitchfork Ben" Tillman in South Carolina. Now African Americans were stigmatized, apparently for good, and so were whites identified with them. Now more than ever it was in whites' interest to distance themselves from blacks. So we find that precisely in counties where residents had questioned slavery before the Civil War and had been Unionists during the conflict, whites now often seemed impelled to prove themselves ultra-Confederate and manifested the most robust anti-black fervor.

Map 3 (page 73) shows places in the nontraditional South that went sundown as a result. Scott County, Tennessee, for example, had been overwhelmingly Unionist, sending 541 men to the United States army and just 19 to the Confederate army. According to county historian Esther Sanderson, "It was their strong nationalism, and not their love of the Negro that led them to fight desperately for the Union. They despised the [slave] system that had relegated them to the status of 'poor mountain whites.' " I believe Sanderson is right: most Appalachian whites were anti-slavery, not pro-black. But Sanderson then goes on to suggest, "An aversion to the Negroes was an aftermath of the war, for many Union men considered slavery the main cause of the war." Here I part company with her, because postwar population statistics in Scott County showed no evidence of "an aversion to the Negroes": 157 African Americans called Scott County home in 1880, and 366 in 1890. Moreover, Scott County voted overwhelmingly (95%) for U.S. Grant for president in 1868, who explicitly favored full rights for African Americans. Scott County did not drive out its African Americans until around 1910, well into the Nadir. By that time, interracial politics were over in Tennessee, at least on the statewide level.[31]

What happened in northwest Alabama is still more graphic. During the Civil War, Winston County famously seceded from the Confederacy and declared itself the "Free State of Winston," whereupon the Confederacy occupied the county by force. Many soldiers from the area deserted from the Confederate Army; some even took the next step and enlisted in the Union Army. After the war, many whites joined the Union League, an organization formed to support the Republican Party and black rights, because former Confederate leaders were still persecuting them. During the Nadir, however, Winston County found it expedient to lose the memory of its anti-slavery past, and while it didn't quite forget that many residents had supported the United States, its contemporary allegiance switched from blue to gray. Steve Suitts grew up in Winston County in the 1950s. On a class visit to Shiloh Battlefield in Tennessee, he bought a blue Civil War cap; his classmates all bought gray, called him a "damned Yankee," and meant it. As part of this switch, most of the county got rid of its African Americans in the 1890s. As late as 2002, except for Haleyville on its western edge, it was not clear that a black family could live peacefully in Winston County.[32]

Many other towns and counties in the nontraditional South that had been Unionist in the 1860s turned Confederate and went sundown at some point after 1890. Myakka City, Florida, for example, inland from Sarasota, had many Union sympathizers during the Civil War, some of whom joined the United States Army, according to local historian Melissa Sue Brewer. After 1890, neo-Confederates seized control and substituted a wholly Confederate past, and in the 1930s, Myakka City banished its African Americans. Although many counties in the Arkansas Ozarks opposed secession and harbored Unionists during the Civil War, every local history I read from Ozark counties, all written around 1890 or thereafter, tells of the war exclusively from the Confederate point of view. Most of these counties expelled their African Americans in the first two decades of the twentieth century. Although not in the Ozarks, Grant County in central Arkansas also had many Unionists during the Civil War; during Reconstruction it was named for one Union general, while Sheridan, its county seat, was named for another. Nevertheless, the Grant County Museum in Sheridan in 2002 had four different Confederate flags for sale and no U.S. flag. Sheridan got rid of its African Americans in 1954. Many counties in north Texas similarly opposed the Confederacy during the Civil War but lost that heritage and drove out their African Americans in the twentieth century.[33]

Hermann, Missouri, on the Missouri River 70 miles west of St. Louis, showed perhaps the most striking transformation in racial ideology of any town in America. Mark Lause, who grew up nearby, notes that Hermann "started as a radical German colony and was an antislavery center in the heart of a slave state." It became the most important Republican stronghold in the state outside of St. Louis. In 1860, Gasconade County, of which Hermann is the seat, cast 52% of its votes for Lincoln, 23% for northern Democrat Stephen A. Douglas, 19% for John Bell, the Constitutional Union candidate, and just 6% for John Breckenridge, the southern pro-slavery candidate, an astonishing proportion for Lincoln in a slave state. After the Civil War, "blacks in the general area used Hermann as the site for celebration of Emancipation Day for a number of years," according to Art Draper of the Gasconade County Historical Society. But, Draper wrote, early in the twentieth century "the German School constituents voted not to integrate the schools," by a margin of just one vote. After that, Hermann's anti-racist idealism collapsed, and the county slid into exclusion. In Draper's words, "The dominant conventional wisdom is that Hermann was a sundown town: 'didn't allow them to stay over night; could come and shop, OK, but don't stay.' " Lause calls this slide "unforgivably pathetic." Gasconade County teaches an important lesson about the power of the anti-black ideology of the Nadir period: if racism could grow to dominate Hermann, with its strong anti-slavery beginnings, it could dominate almost anywhere.[34]

Not every Unionist area in the southern and border states drove out its African Americans. Jones County, Mississippi, had been a center of Unionist activity; as with Winston, Confederates had to occupy it during the war. Jones County did not exclude African Americans. Neither did most counties in West Virginia. We shall see in the next chapter that such intangibles as historical contingency and local leadership made a difference. But even in these areas whites became far more racist during the Nadir than they had been during the Civil War and Reconstruction.

White Ethnic Solidarity

White ethnic group membership also helps to predict which towns would expel their African Americans. Of course, ethnic group membership often went hand in hand with politics, because the Democratic Party appealed more to most white immigrants. But ethnic group membership also made an independent difference, in three ways.

First, ethnic solidarity often led to sundown towns. When ethnic groups came to this country, first-generation immigrants from a country often lived together and worked together. They spoke the same language, shared the same culture, and planned to marry within the group. Often they came from one village in Italy to a village in, say, Vermont, where they quarried granite together, or from one county in Wales to a particular town in Wisconsin. They also banded together for protection from more-established Americans, who often put them down and tried to take advantage of them. Whole towns became overwhelmingly Czech, or German Mennonite, or Italian, sometimes because the town's primary employer—perhaps a coal mine or factory—had recruited its entire labor force from one place in Europe. It was only a short step from this kind of in-group to a town that looked upon any newcomer of a different heritage as an outsider. Such towns were more likely to keep out or drive out African Americans, since they already formed a tight monoethnic in-group. To explain the startling paucity of African Americans in Cedar Falls, Iowa, for example, compared to neighboring Waterloo, historian Robert Neymeyer suggested that Cedar Falls was overwhelmingly Danish, while nearby Waterloo "had a variety of ethnic groups (Germans, Danes, Norwegians, Irish, Italians) with no single dominant force. It was easier for them to accept Croatians, Greeks, Bulgarians, Polish and Russian Jews, and ultimately blacks." My impressionistic comparison of mono- versus multiethnic communities in Texas, Illinois, and elsewhere persuades me that Neymeyer is right: towns with more than one ethnic group were less likely to exclude African Americans than were mono-ethnic towns. Another predictor related to ethnic composition was the sheer size of the black community: African Americans did find some security in numbers.[35]

Second, some white ethnic groups wound up much more anti-black than others. Among mono-ethnic towns, WASP towns—especially elite suburbs—

seem most likely to exclude, particularly after their residual Republican anti-racism wore off in the 1890s. German socialist towns such as Hermann, Missouri, and perhaps Scandinavian and Finnish socialist areas such as Michigan's Upper Peninsula, may also have excluded after their ideological anti-racism wore off. German Lutheran and Catholic towns, Irish towns, Polish towns, and Dutch and German Reformed towns also seem to have gone sundown frequently.

Jews, Italians, and Mexicans were more open, in suburbs and also in neighborhoods within cities. After studying northern cities in the 1920s, T.J. Woofter wrote, "Almost without exception the groups which are most heavily mixed with Negroes in the North are Jewish and Italian. . . . Those least mixed are the Irish and native white people." Even after World War II, according to a long-term black resident of Lancaster, Pennsylvania, police cars served informally as taxis "to take us away from Cabbage Hill, the German neighborhood, when the sun went down," back to the Jewish-Italian-Greek-African American neighborhood that was home.[36]

Across the nation, when African Americans did move to previously white suburbs, often it was to majority Jewish neighborhoods. Unlike WASPs, Jewish Americans lacked the social power to keep blacks out, as Hillel Levine and Lawrence Harmon showed in the Boston area. So when brokers agreed to sell and bankers agreed to make loans to African Americans seeking homes in Jewish neighborhoods, Jews couldn't stop them. Many metropolitan associations of realtors kept out Jewish as well as black agents, making it more likely that Jews and blacks would deal with each other. Also, Jews were not as unified in opposition to blacks as some other ethnic groups. Having faced discrimination based on race themselves, some Jews refused to discriminate. In Detroit, for example, Jews were suspicious of racial covenants, concerned that such provisions might be turned against them. Not only did this make houses available to African Americans, it also undercut public support in Jewish neighborhoods for the kind of violent response that sealed off many other ethnic communities against black would-be pioneers.[37] Consequently, according to historian Charles Bright, "blacks have historically followed the lines of Jewish settlement." The process left most WASP, Irish, and Polish suburbs all-white for decades and helps explain the concentration of African Americans into just a handful of suburbs in each metropolitan area. Ironically, it also confirmed elite WASP suburbs in their anti-Semitism, one reason for which was their fear that "Jews will let blacks in." Evidence in Chapter 14 will suggest that more recently, Mexicans have also been both less willing and less able to keep blacks out. Both of these groups absorbed less of a "white privilege" viewpoint, which came all too easily to other immigrants after they had been in the United States for a decade or two.[38]

The case of Irish Americans merits further discussion. Certainly the Irish faced discrimination throughout the nineteenth century. Often they shared slum neighborhoods and lowly occupations with African Americans. Why, then, did they wind up, in Woofter's words, "least mixed" with blacks, along with WASPs? Writing in 1843, John Finch noted the Irish animosity toward African Americans:

> It is a curious fact that the Democratic Party, and particularly the poorer class of Irish immigrants in America, are greater enemies to the Negro population, and greater advocates for the continuance of Negro slavery, than any portion of the population in the free States.

Finch correctly ascribed Irish racism to *successful* competition. They drove African Americans from occupation after occupation in eastern cities. Then, in the words of Noel Ignatiev, author of *How the Irish Became White,* "To avoid the taint of blackness it was necessary that no Negro be allowed to work in occupations where Irish were to be found. Still better was to erase the memory that Afro-Americans had ever done those jobs."[39]

The third and final point about ethnic group membership is that white ethnic Americans rapidly became "regular" Americans, while African Americans were not allowed to. Even when the Swedish, Italian, Polish, or Greek American newcomers entered as strikebreakers, in competition with older groups, eventually the American part of their identity became more important than the foreign part. Owing to the restrictive 1924 immigration act, new white ethnics grew less common, so the communities of Swedish Americans, Italian Americans, Polish Americans, and Greek Americans grew less Swedish, Italian, Polish, or Greek. White ethnics lost their accents and changed their names. Anders Andersson, prototypical Swedish quarrier, became Michael Anderson, less Swedish and more American. His son in turn never went into the quarry but learned to fix those new horseless carriages and soon ran an automobile dealership. *His* son went to college and became an engineer. Indeed, by the end of the Nadir, around 1940, whites had coalesced as an in-group, except possibly Jews and Mexicans.[40] Soon enough, the only place it mattered that anyone was Swedish American was on public radio's *Prairie Home Companion.*[41] By 2004, an Eastern European name was a source of mild amusement if it was somewhat long, like Brzezinski, but was otherwise regarded as American. So was its bearer—as *white* American.

Even in multiethnic towns, African Americans increasingly served the function of America's primary outgroup, spurring in-group solidarity among whites. Their very presence—or, even better, their mandated absence—by definition grouped all European ethnics as "white." White ethnic groups more and more distanced themselves from African Americans during the Nadir, and even some multiethnic towns went sundown. The history of Granite City, Illinois, across the Mississippi from St. Louis, illustrates the process. Between 1900 and 1910, hundreds of new immigrants, mostly from Macedonia and Bulgaria, poured into Granite City. "Poorly paid, they lived in pathetic squalor, ignorant of American institutions," according to a book published in 1971, Granite City's 75th birthday. Nevertheless, Granite City at least tolerated and sometimes even welcomed these white ethnic group members. They were nonblack, which was more important than being non-American. Precisely at this time, Granite City expelled its African Americans. The white ethnics had started at the bottom, in competition with African Americans, but driving the blacks from Granite City erased that memory over the years. Moreover, when WASP, Irish, Polish, Greek, Italian, and now Macedonian and Bulgarian Americans joined to expel or keep out African Americans around 1903, the whites were now united. No longer could Poles be used against Germans, or Italians against Poles. And no longer could African Americans even live in the community. By 1971, Macedonian American and Bulgarian American children were fully accepted, while African Americans were still totally excluded. Historian Matthew Jacobson showed how whites nationally unified racially during the same period.[42]

Labor Strife

Our discussion of ethnic groups as strikebreakers has brought us to labor strife as an underlying historical and sociological reason for sundown towns. American labor history is replete with the use of outsiders as strikebreakers. Capitalists often used white ethnic groups different from (and lower in status than) their workers who were on strike, because these newer immigrants had little solidarity with the workers whose jobs they were taking. Coal mine owners especially, and on occasion quarry and factory owners, used each successive ethnic group as strikebreakers against the last. In Portland, Connecticut, in the 1870s, for example, Swedes broke into quarrying when Irish and German workers were on strike. Twenty-five years later, Italians did the same thing to the Swedes. Over and over, all across the country, each new group came in as strikebreakers vis-à-vis the former group. Always this generated interethnic animosity.[43]

But when African Americans were the strikebreakers, a special hostility came into play. Having first gotten their toehold in America by being strikebreakers in many cases, white ethnics now reacted venomously to *black* strikebreakers. As historian Ronald Lewis put it, writing about Virden and Pana, Illinois, "Not only were the imports scabs, they were *black* scabs, and the white miners displayed at least as much hostility to their color as to their status as strikebreakers."[44]

Only rarely did the more established group try to expel a white ethnic group en masse. "Whites" in West Frankfort, Illinois, did riot against "Sicilians" in 1920. Historian John Higham describes the scene:

> During the night of August 5, 1920, and all through the following day hundreds of people laden with clothing and household goods filled the roads leading out of West Frankfort, a mining town in southern Illinois. Back in town their homes were burning. Mobs bent on driving every foreigner from the area surged through the streets. Foreigners of all descriptions were beaten on sight, although the Italian population was the chief objective. Time and again the crowds burst into the Italian district, dragged cowering residents from their homes, clubbed and stoned them, and set fire to their dwellings. The havoc went on for three days, although five hundred state troops were rushed to the scene.

Terrible as it was, that scene was less vicious and less permanent than most expulsions of African Americans. Some of the "Sicilians" were willing "to sacrifice their property interests for anything they can get," according to a report in the nearby *Marion Daily Republican.* "Business men are discouraging that practice, assuring all the uneasy that everything will come out all right and they can live here in peace and quiet so long as they are good and loyal citizens." Many returned as soon as the violence died. In the same riot, however, whites forced out all African Americans from West Frankfort. No one made *them* any assurances, and they "went to stay," as a Franklin County history put it succinctly in 1942. In the 2000 census, West Frankfort had not one African American household among its 8,196 people. Similarly, miners in Zeigler drove all Greek Americans out of town at gunpoint and kept them out, but only for two days.[45] Residents of Zeigler told me that African Americans, on the other hand, were still unwelcome as of 2002.[46]

When African Americans were used as strikebreakers, if the strikers won, they typically drove all the black strikebreakers out of town.[47] Often, all other African Americans became fair game at that point—as they sometimes did after a lynching—and the workers simply drove them all out, thus creating a sundown town. In Spring Valley, in northern Illinois, the Italians had come in between 1886 and 1893, recruited by mine owners to depress the wages paid to the French and Belgians who had preceded them. In 1895, the owners used African Americans to threaten the Italian Americans. Late in the evening of August 4, 1895, a mob of more than 800 Italian American miners marched from Spring Valley to the settlement of African American miners two miles west of town, led by the Italian American band as a sort of disguise. "The residents, therefore, remained in their homes and did not react to the oncoming mob," writes historian Felix Armfield, who then quotes the account in the *New York Times*:

> Italians fell upon them like a lot of Apache Indians. Men were dragged from their homes, clubbed, trampled upon, and made targets for the shotguns, rifles, and small arms that the mob had brought with them. The women were insulted, slapped, and two of them, while begging for mercy, were shot down and fatally injured. No one was safe from the mob. Men, women, children, infants, the elderly, and even invalids were attacked.

The rioting continued, and on the second day the Italian miners announced, "The Black Men Must Go." Writing in 1945, historians Arna Bontemps and Jack Conroy summarized, "Nobody knows exactly how many Negroes died before the tumult subsided, but as years went by colored folks, at least, referred to the incident as the 'Spring Valley Massacre.' " The result was the expulsion not only of strikebreakers but of all African Americans in Spring Valley. However, Spring Valley apparently remained sundown only briefly, because African Americans protested statewide and the mine manager insisted on his right to hire black miners.[48]

Similar expulsions took place in Pana and Virden, in central Illinois, in 1898. Miners at four coal mines in Pana had been promised the "Springfield scale," 40 cents per ton, won by miners in nearby Springfield, to take effect April 1, 1898. They had been earning 33 cents. On April 1, the owners reneged, so the workers struck. On May 25, after negotiations, the owners offered 30 cents a ton. So at the next meeting, May 30, the workers demanded 35 cents. On June 29, mine owners announced they would bring in strikebreakers from Alabama. Union miners then surrounded the coal mines with mass picket lines, which kept the mines from opening. Eventually, with the help of police and many ordinary citizens deputized into the police, the owners reopened the mines, using African American labor. On September 28, in the words of Pana historian Millie Meyerholtz, "striking union coal miners and imported Negroes engaged in a pitched battle on the main street. One hundred shots were exchanged." Five blacks and one bystander were hurt; no one was wounded in the union ranks. Both sides then raised the ante. Miners from nearby towns—"heavily armed," according to Meyerholtz—poured into Pana. Hundreds went east, to intercept a train carrying 60 black miners from Indiana.

> The train was flagged down two miles west of Tower Hill by a large company of armed men whose faces were covered by handkerchiefs. The masked men boarded the train and at point of gun, forced men, women, and children to unload. They marched them along the track to Tower Hill. The purpose was to place them on another train and send them back south.

Meanwhile, state militia arrived in Pana on a train with two Gatling guns. September was marked by daily incidents. African Americans were never safe outside of the mine compound. Whites with clubs chased blacks down alleys and through yards and threw rocks at them. Some blacks went back south on trains. "There was a daily passage of insults, slights, and shoves which led to street brawls and secret means of revenge," according to Eleanor Burhorn, who wrote a master's thesis on the event. "Each side antagonized the other." On October 12, whites rioted at the mine in Virden, 40 miles west, where African Americans were also working as strikebreakers. The union had been tipped off that additional black strikebreakers were on their way. When the four-coach train came through Virden, 600 miners lined the tracks and opened a deadly crossfire killing eleven men, including three St. Louis detectives.[49]

On November 15, the Virden owners capitulated to the white miners. Virden has kept out African Americans ever since, although in 2000, it had one black household. On November 25, 1898, Adjutant Gene Reece of the state militia made the wisest analysis of the Pana situation.

> To unionize the blacks is most reasonable to establish the [wage] scale. But the probabilities of its being carried out are few. The bitterness that has been engendered by the union's fight on the Alabama blacks is such, that it is not probable that the blacks would listen to a union man under any circumstances.

Then, too, the race question has entered into the fight to such an extent that it is not likely a movement to get these blacks into the union would meet with favor.

Racism had poisoned the well, making it impossible for black and white miners to drink from any cup of solidarity. On April 10, 1899, a shootout between blacks and whites killed seven people, including a union miner, three black men, a black woman, and a bystander, and wounding fifteen. In June the Pana mine owners admitted defeat too. They closed their mines, stranding their black miners without even train fare to get out of Pana. Eventually 211 African Americans left to go west, perhaps to Kansas and Indian Territory, and 63 went back to Birmingham. Pana also drove out its other blacks, excepting one or two families, as we have seen, and became a sundown town, complete with signs at the edge of town.[50]

Besides Pana and Virden, many other communities trace their origins as sundown towns to a successful strike. Something darker may have happened in Mindenmines, Missouri, where mine operators brought African American strikebreakers to their coal mine in about 1900. Marvin Van Gilder, author of a 1972 history of Barton County, recounts blandly, "Many of them died during their relatively brief residence at the mining camps . . . and a cemetery for the Negro community was established northwest of Mindenmines near the state line." Van Gilder does not explain why or how "many of them died," but Mindenmines became a sundown town upon their demise and probably remains so to this day. According to a staff member at Missouri Southern State College who grew up in the town, a black family moved in for a week in about 1987 and left under pressure; another lived there for about six weeks in about 1990 and left after someone fired a gun at their home. In 2000, Mindenmines was still all-white.[51]

Most shocking of all may be what happened in Zeigler, which has been a sundown town since a series of coal mine explosions between 1905 and 1909 killed dozens of black strikebreakers. Zeigler is a fascinating town, built in concentric circles by its founder, Joseph Leiter, in 1903, who owned its mine. In July 1904, 268 United Mine Workers (UMW) members walked out of the mine on strike. Leiter ordered them out of Zeigler, which he owned, and proceeded to fortify the town. He had an 8-foot-high wooden stockade built, 800 feet long and 400 feet wide, with a live wire on top, enclosing the mine and adjacent territory. Gun turrets were built at each corner of the stockade, and another adorned the roof of the mine office, located in the center of town. Each had a machine gun, and a searchlight mounted on the mine tipple swept the town at night. Strikebreakers came in by train, but the union was often tipped off and opened fire on the trains before they got inside the fortified area. Most strikebreakers quit as soon as they saw the dangerous conditions facing them. Leiter hired more—Italians and others from Europe and African Americans from Kentucky. The strike continued into the winter of 1904–05. "Night after night guns blazed," in the words of Zeigler historian Allan Patton, "bullets ricocheted off of buildings, and dynamite blasts rocked the city." Leiter's fortress held, however, and by spring, many of the striking miners were seeking employment at other mines.[52]

Then on April 3, 1905, the Zeigler mine blew up. Fifty bodies were eventually retrieved, but the remains of some miners were never recovered. The Zeigler mine endured at least three more catastrophes. On November 4, 1908, it had a fire; on January 10, 1909, 26 miners were killed in another explosion; and a third explosion a month later killed three more. Finally Leiter gave up and sold the mine to another owner, who signed with the UMW.

What caused the disasters? The most intriguing account was written in 1953 by Ruby Goodwin, a major figure in neighboring Du Quoin's black community. In her memoir, *It's Good to Be Black,* she tells in detail how a black miner "walked boldly up to the office and applied for a job." He turned out to be "an expert shot firer from upstate" and a union stalwart. "If anyone had been watching they would have seen him climb up the ladder and get into a waiting surrey just a few minutes before the explosion." Goodwin's account intrigues because she is both African American and a devotee of the UMW— for decades the only major union that recruited black members—so she is sympathetic to the murder of 50 to 100 African American miners because it preserved an interracial union. Also, no argument can be made with one statement she makes: "The miners knew that the explosion was not untimely. It was timed to perfection." Unfortunately, neither Patton nor historian Paul Angle, who also treated Zeigler, discuss Goodwin's account.[53] Oral tradition today in the white community in Zeigler and in the black community in Du Quoin agrees with her, holding that the dead miners were mostly black and that one explosion—the first?—was set by union miners.[54] It is this story that Zeigler residents still told me, in 2002, to explain its all-white tradition.[55]

As with ethnicity, labor strife as an underlying cause of sundown towns shares some overlap with politics. Workers—especially union members— were more likely to be Democrats, an alliance that helped make some of them more racist, just as capitalists' alliance with the Republican Party helped make some of them less racist for a time.[56] Indeed, I would argue that racism as a cultural element in the labor movement was more important in causing a town to go sundown than the presence or absence of black strikebreakers as a specific causal variable. Political scientist John Peterson agrees, pointing out that "African American workers joined unions in large numbers whenever they were treated equally." Thus union exclusion usually preceded and facilitated the use of black strikebreakers. In 1894, American Federation of Labor (AFL) head Samuel Gompers allowed unions to join his organization that were white-only, and most AFL unions proceeded to go all-white. As they achieved power during the next 30 years, unions shut blacks out of railroad employment, from construction, and in some places from meatpacking, lumber, and mining as well.[57] After 1900, Gompers repeatedly made racist speeches attacking African Americans, and union workers responded. Often sundown towns resulted.[58]

Of course, not every union town went sundown. Neither did every Democratic or monoethnic town. Not only did the actions taken by local leaders of both races come into play, but so did happenstance—whether something occurred in a given locale to induce white residents to question the right of African Americans (or another minority) to exist in "their" town. The next chapter will explore these immediate "triggers"—catalyzing incidents, usually of real or alleged black misbehavior, sometimes as inoffensive as a black boxing victory a thousand miles away—that prompted whites in a given community to expel its entire black population.

7

Catalysts and Origin Myths

About forty years ago Negroes began to settle in this township in numbers, and it was not long before they became a nuisance. Stealing was rife and all kinds of depredations were going on. Ned Harrigan, who lived here at the time, says that the whites met at the . . . school building, and decided to clear the country of the blacks. A notice was served on the offenders giving them 24 hours to get out of town, and by noon the next day every Negro shanty was empty, and that was the last that was ever heard of them.

—*Chesterton Tribune,* 1903, explaining why and how
that northern Indiana town went all-white[1]

MOST RESIDENTS of the typical sundown town are not good sociologists and never invoke factors such as those given in the previous chapter—political ideology, ethnic makeup, and the like—to explain their town's racial policy. For that matter, the underlying sociological causes do not flatly determine the outcome in a given community. Not every Democratic town expelled its African Americans, although Democratic towns did so far more often than Republican towns. Not every monoethnic town kept blacks out, although monoethnic towns did so more often than multiethnic towns. Not every town with strong white supremacist labor unions drove out *all* its African Americans, although many did. However, as racism intensified during the Nadir, the position of African Americans in towns marked by any or all of these three factors grew so tenuous that the least disturbance—an incendiary remark by a demagogic white politician, news of the next town getting rid of its blacks, a criminal act by a black resident—might set off an expulsion.

What residents of a sundown town often *do* recall is the immediate "reason" why its African Americans were expelled—the trigger. These events play the role of catalysts. If the underlying conditions are right, just as a catalyst in a chemical reaction provides a surface or "hook" enabling the reaction to proceed more rapidly, so the triggering incident provides an excuse or justification for the expulsion or prohibition of African Americans.

In most towns that had African Americans and then had none, some account of this triggering event persists in the local culture to explain their absence. This story then gets raised to the level of myth and becomes used not only as the sole reason for the original expulsion but also to justify the town's continuing exclusion of African Americans.

Labor Strife as Excuse

One underlying cause—organized labor and racialized labor strife—is often cited by residents as the cause of their town's sundown policy. In some towns, however, black strikebreakers were not the real reason for a town going sundown, but only the pretext. This may have been true in Linton, Indiana, for example, which barred all African Americans after a coal company attempted to use black strikebreakers. In the summer of 1903, union miners made a "riotous attack upon the colored waiters at Linton," according to a newspaper account. Linton put up a sundown sign, and all of Greene County, of which Linton is the largest city, went sundown, according to a history teacher who grew up in nearby Vincennes. A black family tried to move into the county in the late 1940s, she said, and "was burned out. No one black would ever *dare* live in Linton," she told me in 2002, and as of the 2000 census, 5,774 people lived in Linton, but there was not one black household.[2] "The colored waiters" had nothing to do with any strikebreakers, however—indeed, nothing to do with mining. White coal miners in Linton were hardly in competition with waiters, so the motivation for the 1903 "riotous attack" wasn't economic. The mining strike seems just an excuse for a more general policy.[3]

As in Linton, workers in Austin, Minnesota, expelled not only black strikebreakers, but all African Americans. In Oshkosh, Wisconsin, according to Andrew Kirchmeier, professor at nearby Ripon College, unions had an agreement with the city, not the employers, to keep African Americans out of town as a matter of municipal policy. Perhaps unions in each city felt that the easiest way to guarantee that black strikebreakers would never trouble them again would be to give their town a reputation for being inhospitable to all African Americans. Or perhaps workers were simply acting on their racist beliefs, shared by their political and labor leaders.[4]

Moreover, unions did not have to be racist to succeed, so it is fallacious to "credit" black strikebreakers with causing a town to go sundown. Labor had examples of nonracist practice, such as Du Quoin, Illinois, where the United

Mine Workers organized an interracial union. There, when managers tried to engage blacks as strikebreakers, unionized African Americans were on hand to dissuade them. The town stayed interracial, the mines stayed organized, and Du Quoin has long been an oasis of racial tolerance compared to its neighboring communities, most of which are sundown towns. It even elected a black alderman in 1918. Thus racism did not flow automatically as a result of social class or union membership.[5]

Some sundown towns invoked labor disputes long after the fact, as an excuse. Miners in Carterville, Illinois, 130 miles south of Pana, faced African American strikebreakers in 1898. Like the mine owners in Pana, Samuel Brush, who operated the biggest mine in Williamson County, just north of Carterville, refused to pay the Springfield scale agreed to by other mine owners with the United Mine Workers. Four-fifths of his workers struck. Brush replaced them with 178 African American miners from Tennessee. Two years of intermittent labor disputes, often marked by violence, followed. On September 17, 1899, some 25 or 30 whites confronted about 15 African Americans at the Illinois Central railroad station and ordered them to get out of town. The blacks started walking up the railroad tracks, with the whites following at a distance. According to historian Paul Angle:

> Suddenly one of the Negroes drew a pistol and fired at the group of pursuers. The miners answered with a volley. Several of the Negroes fell; the others ran for their lives. The whites followed, firing at the fugitives. In a few minutes, not a black man could be seen. Five lay dead; the others, some of them wounded, escaped to the safety of the mining camp.

To this day, some residents of Carterville explain the town's sundown policy by referring to the "black scabs." Historian Herbert Gutman took this position in "The Negro and the UMW." It turns out, however, that Carterville already was a sundown town *before* the importation of the strikebreakers. As Angle noted, Carterville "had long imposed on the Negro a subhuman status. No colored person was permitted even to enter the town."[6]

On the Knife Edge

While black strikebreakers have been wrongly invoked to excuse sundown policies—their actions can never logically justify expelling African Americans who were *not* strikebreakers—nevertheless labor strife does qualify as a catalyst. Often whether a town went sundown came down to such small moments in time as whether a strike was won or lost. If the strikers lost, some striking miners came back to work, joining some of the African American strikebreakers. In the few Pennsylvania towns where African Americans do reside today, "in most cases they are the descendants of strikebreakers," according to Philip Jenkins, author of a study of the Ku Klux Klan in Pennsylvania. Other interracial towns resulting from strikebreakers include Coal Creek, Indiana; Braidwood and Danville, Illinois; Waterloo, Iowa; and Weir City, Kansas. If the union was smart, which the United Mine Workers of America often was, it then organized white and black workers so as not to be undercut by black strikebreakers in the future.[7]

Sometimes a truly insignificant incident made the difference. Mine owner Joseph Leiter was about to sign with the United Mine Workers in a meeting with UMW leaders in Zeigler, Illinois, in June 1904, a month before the strike. Then, in Allan Patton's words:

> According to local legend, John Wesley Shadowen, one of the local [UMW] union officials, made a loud boast of the union conquest of Leiter.[8] Immediately Leiter threw the pen that he held to sign the agreement into the wall and [threw] the contract at Shadowen. In a loud voice Leiter stated that, "Zeigler will run scab forever!"

What if Shadowen had not made his intemperate remark? Then Leiter would have signed with the interracial UMW, and Zeigler might not be a sundown town today.[9]

Other events showed how tenuous was the position of African Americans in towns poised on the knife edge owing to the towns' underlying characteristics. On July 4, 1910, for example, black heavyweight Jack Johnson defeated Jim Jeffries, the "Great White Hope," in Reno, Nevada. African Americans rejoiced in the victory of one of their own, until they came up against the response of white Americans to Jeffries's defeat. Whites attacked African Americans in at least 30 American cities. In Slocum, Texas, they killed 20; all others fled. So Slocum became a sundown town in response to a boxing match more than a thousand miles away. This is what historians call "historical contingency": if Johnson had lost, blacks might have survived in Slocum.[10]

Claims to Equality Led to Sundown Towns

The real reason that Jack Johnson's victory led to at least one sundown town and to many attacks on African American neighborhoods was that he demonstrated that blacks could be the equal of whites, at least in the boxing ring. During the Nadir, that was a dangerous claim for an African American to make. Indeed, Johnson boldly maintained that he was socially equal to whites as well, openly dating and marrying white women. Whites have often been un- willing to concede that African Americans might be their equal in wealth, so- cial status, or even more minor skills such as boxing or poker, and their anger at the possibility often triggered sundown towns.

Whites might claim to be upset by problematic African Americans— criminals and ne'er-do-wells—but more frequently they lashed out at those who were industrious and successful, for it was these families whose existence set up a claim to social and economic equality. Such claims underlay the ex- pulsion by white Democrats of about 200 African Americans from Washing- ton County, Indiana, shortly after the Civil War. The earliest victim of the violence was John Williams, "who had acquired a farm and an unusual amount of wealth for a Negro," in the words of historian Emma Lou Thorn- brough. "In December, 1864, he was shot to death in his own dooryard. In 1867 there was another murder, the victim being an inoffensive old man who had aroused the ire of some of his white neighbors by persisting in attending their church, even after he had been warned to stay away." These and other terrorist actions led to an exodus, and Washington County remained all-white until 1990. To achieve wealth or attend church implied that African Ameri- cans were the social equals of whites, which these Indiana whites would not tolerate.[11]

In the larger riots for which we have more information, such as the 1908 attempt in Springfield, Illinois, and the 1921 attempt in Tulsa, Oklahoma, to cleanse these cities of African Americans, we can see the same dynamic at work. Margaret Ferguson, an African American trying to avoid the mob in Springfield, pointed out, "There was a great deal of animosity toward any well-established Negro who owned his own house and had a good job." Riot- ers there specifically targeted William Donnegan, an elderly African Ameri- can who had been Abraham Lincoln's cobbler. His sin, besides his race itself, was that he was prosperous, and also that he had been married to a white woman for over 30 years. The mob cut his throat and hanged him. "They were very busy hurting the prominent," Ferguson wrote later, "and so of course we were frightened, you see, because we, also, were affluent." In Tulsa, too, whites particularly targeted successful middle-class families.[12]

Sometimes the affront may seem trivial until we recognize that a claim for equality was involved. In Owosso, in central Michigan, on October 4, 1871, African American residents held a party, complete with an Italian band. Some white residents apparently tried to crash it, and the African Americans said they were not welcome, since blacks had been ejected from a white masquerade ball some months earlier.[13] An argument ensued; the blacks ousted the whites and beat them on the street. The white community returned en masse and forced all African Americans[14] out of town.[15]

Sometimes direct economic competition between small-business owners engaged in the same trade played a role. In 1892, when whites in Norman, Oklahoma, first drove out their black residents, an African American named Doll Smith, a barber, received a note of warning:

> You are hereby notified to leave this town in the next ten days. We are determined that no "niggers" shall live in this town. We give you timely warning to get your things and "git" or you must stand the consequences.

Smith did leave, and nine months later, when whites forced the black residents of nearby Lexington to flee, a white barber, George Elkins, played a leading role. In Lexington, according to the *Guthrie [Oklahoma] News,* "Negro men were tied up and beaten, and Negro women outraged." Federal District Court indicted twenty whites, but the cases were continued for a year and finally dismissed.[16]

In November 1920, African Americans in Ocoee, Florida, west of Orlando, made a still more serious claim to equality: they tried to vote. A Republican judge, John Cheney, facilitated their registration, which outraged white Democrats, who dominated much of Orange County. The "Grand Master Florida Ku Klucks" sent the following notice to Judge Cheney:

> If you are familiar with the history of the days of Reconstruction which followed in the wake of the Civil War, you will recall that the "Scallawags" [*sic*] of the North, and the Republicans of the South proceeded very much the same as you are proceeding, to instill into the Negro the idea of social equality. You will also remember that these things forced the loyal citizens of the South to organize clans of determined men, who pledged themselves to maintain white supremacy and to safeguard our women and children.
>
> And now if you are a scholar, you know that history repeats its self, and that he who resorts to your kind of a game is handling edged tools. We shall always enjoy WHITE SUPREMACY in this country and he who interferes must face the consequences.

On election day, two prosperous African American landowners in Ocoee, Mose Norman and Julius Perry, went to the polls. Democratic officials turned them away. Norman returned later with a shotgun, insisting that he be allowed to vote. "An altercation ensues," in the words of Bianca White, co-director of a documentary film on the incident, "and Mose Norman is pistol whipped and sent away a second time. Mose Norman is never heard from again." Colonel Sam Salisbury then organized a lynch mob to punish Norman and Perry for trying to vote. By nightfall, white residents of Ocoee, joined by more than 250 Klansmen from around the state, collected in the town and attacked its black neighborhoods. More than 300 African Americans fled for their lives "into the orange groves, swamps, and neighboring towns." Many were burned in their homes or shot as they fled them. Twenty-five homes, two churches, and a Masonic lodge were incinerated; the death toll was between 8 and 60. Perry's body was found hanging from a light pole the next morning. For nearly a week deputized Klansmen held the city. They divvied up the land owned by African Americans and sold it for $1.50 an acre. Ocoee stayed all-white until 1981.[17]

Until 1921, residents of Montlake, then a small coal mining town, now a suburban area near Soddy-Daisy in East Tennessee, drew their water from a centrally located spring, "the only one available for general use," according to an article in the *Chicago Defender,* the nation's premier black newspaper. As segregation drew stricter during the Nadir, whites grew less willing to countenance the equality of status implied by sharing a spring. "The prejudice of the whites had made them try to keep any one but themselves from using the spring," in the *Defender*'s words. "On several occasions individuals have had fights over the water, and, in a number of instances, the whites have been worsted. It is felt that this condition led to the circulation of reports that if anything should happen again the whites were going to band together to force the other residents from their homes." At this point a black girl, eight-year-old Jewel Flipper, went to the spring for water. Four white girls apparently stopped her. An altercation ensued, and in the aftermath, whites drove out the entire African American population—some 60 miners and their families. "After driving them out the whites guarded the streets, went into the cabins and took all of value, and kept any one from entering the town by way of the roads." Decades later, according to oral history, Soddy-Daisy sported a sign that said "Niggers' Fun, Look and Run."[18]

Threat of School Desegregation Led to Sundown Towns

School desegregation presented a similar claim of equality. We saw that school desegregation was involved in Hermann, Missouri, which proved unable to